Anyone who eats (or cooks) a gluten-free diet understands the struggles of avoiding gluten.

In East Asian and Southeast Asian foods especially, gluten is hard to avoid: it's embedded in integral staples like soy sauce and gochujang and foundational foods like noodles and dumplings. But the struggle is over! In *My Best Friend Is Gluten-Free*, you'll find completely gluten-free recipes that celebrate a spectrum of Asian flavors.

Inspired by her celiac husband and wanting to share the foods of her Chinese-Canadian upbringing with him, Jannell Lo set out to create gluten-free options for all her favorite recipes, plus some creative takes of her own. Designing flavorful and inclusive dishes let Jannell explore her own cultural identity through food in new and meaningful ways. The result: this cookbook, with chapters that include salads and fresh bites in Tossed & Assembled, satisfyingly saucy pairings in Nice with Rice, crispy stir-fries in Fried & Sizzled, and easy Sweet Treats with textural flair.

My Best Friend Is Gluten-Free is exciting for all eaters, gluten-free or not, with:

- **Gluten-Free Solutions to Asian Classics:** For anyone feeling left out at restaurants, find GF answers to Canto-Style Mapo Tofu, Japanese-Style Curry, and Hot & Sour Soup.
- **Barrier-Breaking Recipes:** Cross culinary borders—think Thai, Chinese, Filipino—with Tom Yum Corn Chowder, Shanghai Stir-Fried Gnocchi, and Pavlova with Calamansi Curd inspired by Jannell's travels as a third-culture chef.
- **Easy Everyday Meals for All Dietary Needs:** Whip up weeknight wins like Rice Cake Soup, Chili Miso Salmon, and Roasted Coconut Tamari Chicken, with many plant-based, vegetarian, dairy-free, and pescatarian options!
- **Menus for All Occasions:** Serve your friends and family multi-course menus, like a cozy holiday feast, a Lunar New Year dinner, and even a sumptuous plant-based spread.

With eye-catching illustrations and vibrant photos, *My Best Friend Is Gluten-Free* is an accessible and fun exploration of a world typically off-limits to gluten-free eaters. Finally, you can make your favorite Asian dishes at home.

MY BEST FRIEND IS GLUTEN-FREE

100+ Asian-Inspired Recipes for Bringing People Together

JANNELL LO

appetite
by RANDOM HOUSE

Appetite by Random House® and colophon are
registered trademarks of Penguin Random House LLC.

Library and Archives Canada Cataloguing in Publication
is available upon request.

ISBN: 978-0-525-61278-0
eBook ISBN: 978-0-525-61279-7

Book and cover design by Dylan Browne and Joannza Lo
Typeset by Sean Tai
Illustrations by Joannza Lo on pages i, iii, v, vii, ix, 1, 6, 10,
22, 23, 26, 31, 32, 33, 68, 69, 94, 95, 128, 129, 166, 167, 202,
203, 234, 240, 243, 244, and 254
Illustrations by Nancy Pappas on pages 11–21

Printed in Malaysia

The authorized representative in the EU for product
safety and compliance is Penguin Random House
Ireland, Morrison Chambers, 32 Nassau Street,
Dublin D02 YH68, Ireland. https://eu-contact.penguin.ie

Published in Canada by Appetite by Random House®,
a division of Penguin Random House Canada Limited.
320 Front Street West, Suite 1400
Toronto Ontario, M5V 3B6, Canada

www.penguinrandomhouse.ca

10 9 8 7 6 5 4 3 2 1

appetite   Penguin
by RANDOM HOUSE   Random House
             Canada

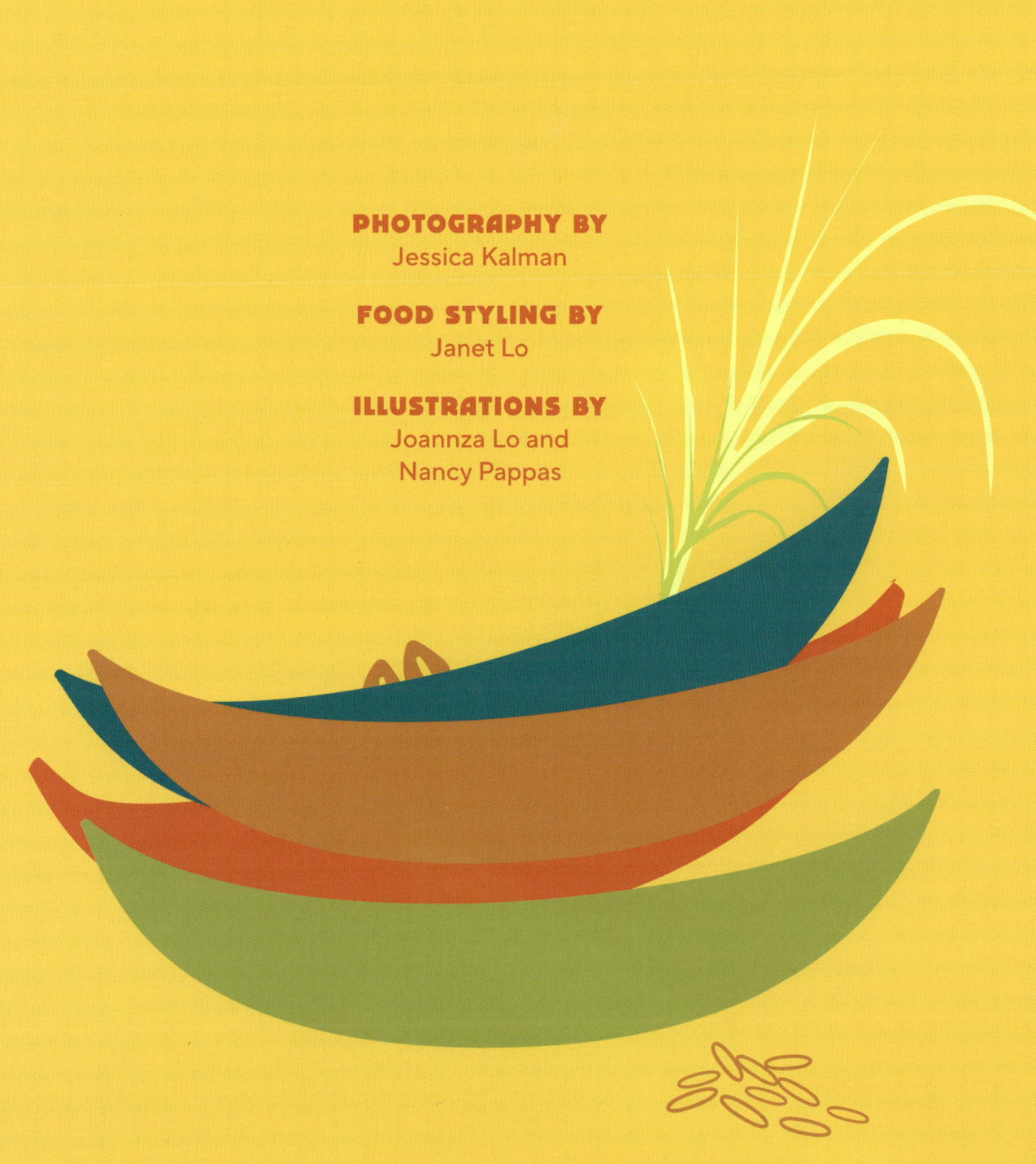

PHOTOGRAPHY BY
Jessica Kalman

FOOD STYLING BY
Janet Lo

ILLUSTRATIONS BY
Joannza Lo and
Nancy Pappas

To my friends and fam, who have
supported me through this wild ride.

And to Best Friend, Reid, my kick-ass
cooking partner and other half,
this book is as much yours as it is mine.

CONTENTS

INTRODUCTION

For the first 20 years of my life, I juggled two identities. At home, I was Chinese. At school, I was Canadian. When I stepped into professional kitchens, Western cuisines took center stage, leaving little room for the flavors that had shaped my childhood. I craved a space where my dual identity wasn't just accepted but celebrated—a space where I could be unabashedly Jannell, revealing the layers that make up who I am. This desire drove me to find a deeper connection to my identity through cooking my own food, blending the influences of my upbringing with the skills I honed in professional kitchens.

Meeting Reid, whose curiosity about Chinese cuisine mirrored my own passion for culinary exploration, reminded me of the rich tapestry of my experiences as a Chinese-Canadian gal from Toronto, and the importance of sharing those flavors and stories with others. I no longer wanted to hide behind foods that my friends had taught me were "easy to like"—pizza, pasta, and pancakes are great, but they never brought me comfort the way a bowl of saucy mapo tofu or congee do.

So much of my family's time together was spent over food. Whether it was watching my grandma make glutinous rice dumplings, tending to my grandpa's winter melons in the yard, or feasting with my parents at the best Chinese seafood restaurants across Toronto, food expressed love when there wasn't the vocabulary to express it through words. From healing soups to elaborate hot pot meals, my parents strived to give my sisters and me a life of abundance, joy, and security.

When Reid and I met, it was clear that he came from the same school of food-as-love that I did. Because of his early-childhood diagnosis of celiac, Reid's mom spent hours in the kitchen adjusting her recipes to fit his diet, and he came to see all her work as a pure expression of love. Following her example, he learned his way around a kitchen out of necessity and discovered an appreciation for eating, cooking, and sharing these dishes with loved ones. Both Reid and I had our own version of the desire to belong, particularly within the context of food as a means of connection.

The difficulty was highlighted when we began to navigate his gluten allergy together. Reid was used to navigating the gluten-free world of the Western foods he had grown up with, but it was now, when I was keen on taking him out for dim sum, that we came to roadblocks. I realized that many Asian condiments contain sneaky traces of gluten (wheat flour in soy sauce, miso paste, and gochujang, to name a few), and suddenly noodles and dumplings (foundational foods!) were off-limits. With my growing experience in professional kitchens, I was determined to find ways to share my food culture with Reid, and conjointly, we entered a new world of culinary possibilities.

Grandpa's (Gong Gong's) rice rinsing ritual

We spent hours scouring shops to find gluten-free versions of essential condiments. The seemingly straightforward task of grocery shopping became a meticulous label-reading expedition with stops at multiple stores. We combined Asian flavors I grew up eating with locally available ingredients, finding an intersection of cultures that resonated with me.

As a chef of color navigating the culinary landscape of North America, this approach to food liberated me from the fear of criticism for cooking "inauthentically." The pressure for non-Western cuisines to stay strictly "authentic" can hinder chefs of color from creating outside the box because we are made to feel like incorporating unexpected ingredients into traditional dishes is sacrilegious. However, it can be done tactfully by giving credit where it's due. For me, this liberation has manifested as experimenting with gluten-free ingredients and surprising flavor combinations. The food I create is my life on a plate—a representation of my cross-cultural history and

diverse influences, allowing me to honor meaningful traditions while adding my own touch, and finding a way to share it all with Reid.

Believing that there must be others on a similar journey, in 2016 I created *My BF Is GF* (short for My Best Friend Is Gluten-Free), a food blog documenting our gluten-free creations. Jump to the present day, and this cookbook is here to change the narrative on gluten-free foods. It's a vibrant collection of recipes inspired by my third culture identity, ensuring that even people with celiac can enjoy Asian flavors. Beyond expanding the realm of gluten-free eats, this book is about breaking cultural culinary barriers and embracing the freedom to create outside the box. It's a balance I consistently aim for in my work with food; too often, gluten-free eating is associated with diets that put the joy of eating on the back burner, but that's not the case here.

Within these pages, you'll discover playful and adaptable recipes that offer creative solutions for cooking East Asian and Southeast Asian–inspired foods in the West for a range of dietary palates. These blended recipes embrace the term "fusion" by using a mix of cuisines inspired by my experience growing up Chinese in the multicultural city of Toronto and family travels around the world. I don't claim ownership over any particular cuisine, acknowledging the delicate balance of navigating diverse influences. Each recipe is a heartfelt attempt to ensure that those with gluten allergies or a limited pantry can savor these flavors and capture the essence of certain traditional dishes. While the substitutes may not be clones of their gluten-filled counterparts, the goal is for everyone, gluten-free or not, to enjoy

Grandma (Poh Poh) and me

them. I've included "inspired by" notes in each recipe that pay homage to the people and places that shaped it, sharing the story behind its creation.

THIS APPROACH TO FOOD LIBERATED ME FROM THE FEAR OF CRITICISM FOR COOKING "INAUTHENTICALLY."

To make navigating the recipes easier, each one also has handy dietary labels, allowing you to quickly identify whether it's suitable for your diet. And starting on page 238, you'll find the recipes sorted by these needs. If any adjustments are needed to make the recipe meet the dietary need, these are noted under an "Option" head above the ingredient list. Here's a rundown of what each icon means:

 **DAIRY-FREE OR DAIRY-FREE OPTION**

PLANT-BASED OR PLANT-BASED OPTION

VEGETARIAN OR VEGETARIAN OPTION

PESCATARIAN OR PESCATARIAN OPTION

On page 234, you'll also find suggested menus using my recipes. Whether for a casual get-together or a festive celebration, these menus showcase the versatility of gluten-free Asian-inspired meals.

Since music is another memory-maker, I've included scannable QR codes at the beginning of each chapter to songs that transport me to the times I ate or created a dish. You'll get a peek into my world with the opportunity to create memories of your own. If you want to listen through all the songs that keep me dancing in the kitchen or bopping at a dinner party, scan this code:

Scan me to
listen along!

Iron Chef Chen Kenichi for Halloween

My hope is that this book empowers you to create both comforting and exciting dishes that celebrate the multifaceted layers of Asian identity for a spectrum of dietary needs. Whether you're seeking to embrace your own cultural heritage, expand your culinary repertoire, or simply enjoy delicious meals with friends and family, *My Best Friend Is Gluten-Free* is here to revolutionize your kitchen. It's a gateway to self-expression, joy, and unity through modern gluten-free Asian cooking.

Thank you so much for being here. It truly means the world.

Jannell

A NOTE FROM BEST FRIEND

I have celiac.

What's that?

Celiac disease. I can't eat gluten.

Gluten?

Do you know what wheat is?

No . . .

My conversations with servers have evolved over the years from that original script from 1995, but it often remains frustrating and demoralizing to eat out. These days, gluten-free menus ease the pain, freeing me from the "if onlys" that censor my dreams of fried foods and giving me a sense of security that the servers at least know what gluten is (not long ago that wasn't always the case!). But restaurants with alternate menus remain a relative rarity.

My unsuccessful attempts at eating out meant that I didn't experiment much with food when I was growing up. Even before being diagnosed at the age of four, I wasn't very adventurous. My favorite foods were toast and Cheerios, and because I was so malnourished from undiagnosed celiac, I was given free rein to indulge in my desires. After the diagnosis, I was afraid of new foods, intimidated by the need to read the ingredients of everything I ate and paranoid about spending the night sick after getting glutened (again) at the hands of a well-meaning stranger or loved one.

There were a few cuisines that gave me some respite: Thai curries were a stalwart friend, Indian restaurants were mostly safe spaces, and tacos have always been a source of great joy. But many foods from around the world remained inaccessible. Fast food is by and large held by the gluten; East Asian food is friendly on the surface, with its predilection for rice, but most dishes feature fermented bean pastes full of undercover gluten; European restaurants were largely a no; and even Thai food was suspect outside of my beloved curries. The list goes on.

All that to say that I was comfortable in my lane and didn't seek novelty in my diet. I wanted safety and security—bacon and eggs or my mom's grilled mustard chicken with steamed broccoli and rice pilaf (still a favorite in Jannell's and my home). I loved to eat, but I feared new things.

Now, this wouldn't be a story if things didn't change, and the story wouldn't belong in this book if Jannell weren't the agent of change.

Everything changed when I met Jannell.

Jannell never makes me feel like my diet is a burden to be managed; instead, it's an interesting set of boundaries within which to experiment. From the beginning, she has gone the extra mile to create spaces where I fit in. She has simultaneously pushed my boundaries and kept me comfortable, transforming me from a picky eater to a curious and enthusiastic one.

JANNELL'S FOOD EMBODIES HER SPIRIT: INCLUSIVE AND PLAYFUL, RESPECTFUL WITHOUT BEING DOGMATIC.

Gluten-free food has recently become linked with diet culture. It gets lumped in with keto, paleo, and vegan diets, and is associated in pop culture with tanned Beverly Hills types searching for the next way to lose 10 pounds. Jannell cooks from a different place. She cooks from joy and love, with a sense of indulgence tempered by moderation and balance. Her food embodies her spirit: inclusive and playful, respectful without being dogmatic. She loves and celebrates everything from fresh and revitalizing meals to deeply satisfying hearty dishes that will sustain you through the winter. From a gluten eater who cooks gluten-free, Jannell's food is never just "great for being gluten-free." Forget everything you know about "for being gluten-free"—this book eschews the qualifier. The food is simply great.

It's hard to trust other people to cook for you when you have allergies, but Jannell is so thoughtful and meticulous that it's easy to feel safe in her hands. She reads ingredients as thoroughly as I do, she calls restaurants ahead to negotiate beforehand so I never have to wallow in uncertainty, and she has introduced me to foods I would never have experienced without her. She has broadened my horizons immensely, allowing me to experience the same joy of discovery, the same thrill of novelty, that comes so easily to the fortunate among us with no restrictions on their diet. She has replaced my fear with delight. And I am so excited for you to experience that same joy as you eat your way through this book.

Happy eating!

Reid

Prepping for a pop-up in Toronto.

JLO'S KITCHEN TOOLS

Great meals can be made with basic tools, but let me show you my lineup of helpful kitchen tools that are totally worth investing in. While some of these are more "nice-to-haves," they'll make your life in the kitchen much more manageable, making you a more confident and mindful cook.

BLENDER

A high-power blender, such as a Vitamix, is my top pick of stand blenders for its ability to blend anything from sauces to smoothies into a velvety consistency.

DUTCH OVEN

A heavy-duty enameled cast-iron pot that seamlessly transfers from the stovetop to the oven. I use my Le Creuset regularly for soups, stews, and braises. When paired with a steamer rack or bamboo basket, it also becomes a convenient way to cook dumplings or reheat leftovers (see sidebar on page 8). Our first Dutch oven lasted about 10 years with heavy use.

FOOD PROCESSOR

A total time-saver for big chopping, grating, and mixing jobs, such as for the salmon burger patties on page 159.

GRILL

Throughout this book, when I mention grilling, I'm referring to using an outdoor gas grill, which I prefer for its simple temperature control compared to that of a charcoal grill. For added flexibility, most grilling recipes also include an oven-roasting alternative.

IMMERSION BLENDER

An immersion blender is a handheld blender, convenient for submerging directly into pots for a speedy blitz. Use it to whip up fresh mayonnaise or small batches of dressings in the handy cylindrical cup it comes with.

INSTANT-READ THERMOMETER

The best way to achieve perfectly cooked meat is to use an instant-read thermometer. My ThermoPop never leaves my knife bag when I travel, and it comes in a fun range of colors. Aim for these temps when cooking meat:

- 135°F (57°C): medium-rare steaks
- 145°F (63°C): pork
- 160°F (71°C): chicken

After it reaches the required temperature, be sure to let the meat rest for at least 5 minutes to kill off bacteria: cover it with foil on a cutting board, let the meat rest, and remove the foil before slicing. This rest is especially important when cooking chicken: you might have read that you should cook chicken to 165°F (74°C), but if you let it rest properly after cooking it to 160°F (71°C), you'll kill off the bacteria and still get really juicy meat.

KITCHEN SCALE

An essential tool to get precise measurements. I've included weights for packaged ingredients and for baking, where accurate measurements are important. I also love a scale for portioning out an exact amount of pasta every time.

MANDOLINE

Ask anyone who has worked in a restaurant kitchen, and they'll tell you that the Benriner mandoline with the iconic bowl-cut lady on the box is the most reliable mandoline. It comes with three attachments for various thin julienne cuts, as well as a hand guard for safer slicing. I whip mine out for tasks like shredding cabbage, thinly slicing cucumbers, and julienning carrots. It's the not-so-secret secret to great slaws and pickles.

MICROPLANE ZESTER

The best tool for zesting citrus and grating spices, and for mincing ginger and garlic.

PRESSURE COOKER

Whether it's a stovetop model or an Instant Pot, a pressure cooker boils water at 250°F (120°C), which means it dramatically shortens the time needed for braises compared to simmering on the stove or in the oven, while delivering equally impressive results.

RICE COOKER

I hate picking favorites, but this might be our most important piece of kitchen equipment. Rice is life—especially in a gluten-free Asian diet! It might be a one-trick pony, but if you eat a lot of rice, like we do,

> ### LET'S TALK ABOUT HOT SPOTS
> Some areas in your oven or grill may run hotter in temperature than others. Get to know them! Rotate dishes halfway through roasting or move food around on the grill for even cooking and coloring.

this device will change your life. Basic models work perfectly well, but we love our Tiger 3-cup rice cooker with its specialty functions for "quick" and "brown rice" cooking.

SALAD SPINNER

People often sleep on the salad spinner, but it's your gateway to truly dry herbs and veggies for deliciously crisp salads and slaws (such as Crisp Cabbage Slaw, page 51).

STAND MIXER

It takes up quite a bit of counter space, but if you're a passionate baker, I recommend a stand mixer. It makes forming doughs a breeze, like for my Miso Tahini Cookies (page 226) and Black Sesame Buttermilk Loaf (page 218).

TOASTER OVEN

If you've got a mix of gluten and gluten-free eaters in your home, I highly recommend upgrading to a toaster oven. Most come with a removable catcher tray, making it easy to clean up crumbs (to get those micro glutens out of there!). You can also use them for small roasting jobs, like vegetables, or reheating pizza when you don't have time or energy for your oven. We love our Cuisinart model, which is large enough for a small frozen pizza—gluten-free, of course.

WOK (NONSTICK)

This is a really hot take, but I suggest starting with a nonstick wok over a carbon steel one. For home cooks, the ease of cooking, maintaining, and cleaning is more valuable than the ability to cook over scorching high heat, which is what a carbon steel wok allows. To keep the nonstick surface pristine, avoid cooking on higher than medium-high heat and opt for utensils made of wood or bamboo—anything but metal, which can scratch off the coating. Of course, you can always graduate to a carbon steel wok once you've mastered the basics, but until then, you can achieve satisfying results with a nonstick wok.

SETTING UP YOUR STEAMER

Here's how to best steam food like dumplings or leftovers to retain flavor and prevent food from drying out:

1. You'll need a wide pot (a Dutch oven works great) with a steamer rack, or one suitable for a bamboo steamer basket to rest in without touching the bottom. Fill the pot with 1½ to 2 inches of water, ensuring it doesn't touch the vessel holding your food, and bring it to a boil.

2. Prepare a heatproof bowl (Corelle is Ma's pick) with the food you want to heat. Place the bowl directly on the steamer rack or inside the bamboo steamer and cover it with the pot lid or bamboo steamer lid.

3. Reduce the heat to medium-high, and let the steam heat the food for 6 to 10 minutes, depending on how much you've got in there. To check if the food is ready, insert a spoon or fork in the center and taste—use your senses!

4. Use a dry kitchen towel or specific tongs used for retrieving hot dishes from a steamer (found in Asian supermarkets, kitchenware stores, or on Amazon) to carefully take out the hot vessel.

5. Before enjoying your meal, transfer the hot food to a separate plate, or place the hot dish on a trivet to protect the table surface.

GLUTEN-FREE ASIAN PANTRY

These ingredients are the heart and soul of the book, and if you peek into my fridge or pantry at any given moment, they are largely what you'd find. They're the essentials I can't live without, the flavor builders that transform dishes, and they absolutely deserve a place in your kitchen too. (Of course, if you're not GF, you can use standard versions of these products!) If you have trouble finding some of the items, you don't have to miss out! I've provided substitutions with ingredients that are easier to find or that you probably already have in your pantry.

For those of you just diving into the world of celiac and gluten-free living, it's essential to steer clear of wheat, barley, rye, or spelt. Wheat, the most prevalent and low-cost form of gluten, frequently appears in East and Southeast Asian dishes, where noodles and dumplings abound and staple condiments are made with wheat flour to speed up their fermentation process. But no worries—I've got easy-to-find substitutes, so you can whip up gluten-free Asian eats without breaking a sweat. For ingredients that often contain gluten, I've listed brands that are confirmed to be gluten-free (like San-J for tamari); for ingredients that are naturally gluten-free, I've suggested some of my favorite brands (for coconut milk, for instance, I like Aroy-D, which doesn't contain added emulsifiers).

Please note that some of these ingredients, while free of gluten, may not be certified gluten-free. Some of the brands also have gluten versions of the same items, so be sure to read all labels before consuming an ingredient. You'll find most of these essentials at your local Asian grocery store, at large supermarket chains, or online, through the usual big retailers.

ANCHOVIES
Flavor: briny, funky, umami

The key to building deep, savory flavor in salad dressings, sauces, soups and stews. Opt for anchovies in glass jars over cans for easier storage. *Plant-based substitute: An equal amount of finely chopped capers or kalamata olives can add a similar brininess to your dish.*

CHILI CRISP OR OIL
Flavor: spicy, roasty, salty, savory
GF brands: Lao Gan Ma, Zing, Fly by Jing, Super Magic Taste, MìLà, Bowlcut, Holy Duck, Boon

There are few things I wouldn't add chili crisp to for a boost of spice and umami. Lao Gan Ma is the most widely available, but look for their Spicy Chili Crisp made with soybeans, since some of their other chili oil products contain gluten. Not all chili oils are gluten-free, as some contain soy sauce.

CHILIES
Flavor: spicy, vegetal, fruity

Since fresh chilies often come in packs that are far too large for the average home cook, keeping them frozen in a storage bag (for up to 6 months) is a convenient way to have them on hand for adding heat to spicy dishes. I usually stock long red Thai chilies, which are moderately spicy (15,000 to 30,000 Scoville heat units). Opt for fresh chilies when preparing cold dishes.

CHILI PASTE
Flavor: spicy, tangy, peppery, salty
Favorite brand: Huy Fong Foods

The iconic maker of sriracha, Huy Fong Foods makes a chili paste (sambal oelek) that is also extremely popular. It's what I reach for when I want to add a last-minute kick to a dish. They have a chili garlic sauce in almost identical packaging, and either product works well for the recipes in this book.
Substitute: An equal amount of Calabrian chili paste; or harissa: start with ½ the amount and increase to taste, as harissa pastes can vary in spice

CHINESE BLACK VINEGAR
Flavor: tangy, malty, smoky
GF brands: Patchun, Great Wall, Uchibori

It can also be called black rice vinegar, Chinkiang vinegar, Zhenjiang vinegar, or Japanese aged rice vinegar (kurozu). If you can't find the brands above, be especially careful to check the ingredients list: black rice vinegar can contain wheat from the fermentation process. Look for a dark vinegar made from glutinous rice, millet, or sorghum.
Substitute: A 1:1 mix of balsamic and rice vinegars, or the same amount of balsamic

CILANTRO
Flavor: bright, refreshing

To extend the life of cilantro for up to a month, cut an inch off the stems, then submerge in a glass with about 2 inches of water, cover it all with a produce bag, and place in the fridge. Buy bunches without yellow or wilted leaves, change the water every week, and rinse and spin as needed. Use this method for dill, mint, and parsley, too.
Substitute: An equal amount of culantro (sawtooth herb) or parsley

COCONUT MILK AND CREAM
Flavor: creamy, rich, sweet
Favorite brands: Aroy-D, Cha's, Chaokoh, Savoy (cream only)

Look for canned coconut milks (not the ones in cartons used as a dairy milk alternative) that don't contain an added emulsifier like guar gum. Without the guar gum, it naturally separates into coconut cream and coconut water when left unshaken. You can use coconut cream for frying up aromatics in stir-fries, due to its high fat content, and the water is ideal for braises or for cooking rice.

COOKING OIL
Flavor: neutral, vegetal

Use canola, avocado, grapeseed, safflower, sunflower, vegetable, or refined olive oils with smoke points of 400°F (200°C) or higher for high-heat cooking—including sautéing, searing, frying, grilling, or roasting.

COOKING WINE OR SAKE

Flavor: boozy, yeasty, rice
GF brands: Shirakiku, Wangzhihe, Pearl River Bridge

Many Chinese recipes call for Shaoxing wine, which often contains wheat. If you can't find one that's made purely from rice, cooking-grade sake works just as well. My recipes call for the unsalted kind; if you can only find salted, adjust the salt in the recipe to taste.
Substitute: An equal amount of dry sherry

CORNSTARCH

To make a cornstarch slurry for thickening stews and sauces, use a 1:1 ratio of cornstarch to cold water. Store cornstarch in plastic tubs; it's less messy than the boxed kind and totally refillable from the bulk store.
Substitute: An equal amount of potato starch

CURRY PASTE

Flavor: spicy, aromatic, floral, pungent
Favorite brands: Maesri, Aroy-D, Mae Ploy, Cock

Maesri is our top choice for Thai curry pastes. Their gluten-free options include green, massaman, red, and panang. Their yellow curry paste is not gluten-free. Any extra paste can be frozen flat in a food storage bag for up to 3 months and broken off in pieces as needed.
Plant-based note: Check for seafood products.

EXTRA VIRGIN OLIVE OIL

Flavor: peppery, fruity, herbaceous

Treat yourself to a nice, fruity mid-range EVOO (it doesn't need to break the bank) for drizzling over cold dishes only. I never heat up EVOO, as it has a low smoke point of 325°F (165°C). I love drizzling it over my food; when the recipes call for a drizzle, that's about 1 to 4 teaspoons. If your EVOO doesn't come with a narrow spout, transfer it to a squeezy bottle for easy drizzling.

FISH SAUCE
Flavor: fishy, umami, pungent, salty
Favorite brands: Red Boat, Megachef, Squid

Used to bump up the salt and umami in any dish. Squid is a widely available, affordable brand that gets the job done, but it's worth splurging on Red Boat or Megachef for well-rounded flavor. Double-check the ingredients in other brands, as some are not gluten-free.
Plant-based substitute: An equal amount of GF soy sauce or tamari

FRIED GARLIC AND SHALLOTS
Flavor: roasty, aromatic, nutty
GF brands: Cock, Maesri, JHC, Dragonfly

A convenient way to add savory flavor and crunch to your dishes. The best ones use only the basic ingredients—shallots or garlic, oil, and salt, but always check for wheat flour.

GARLIC
Flavor: pungent, robust, savory

Look for fresh garlic with plump, firm cloves. Keep an eye out for solo garlic at the farmers market, which comes as a single clove head equal to about four average cloves, making it much easier to peel. Store for up to 3 months in a dark, dry place. For roasting, use garlic powder, as it coats food well and doesn't burn as easily.
Substitute: ⅛ tsp garlic powder per clove of garlic

GINGER
Flavor: warm, spicy, earthy

Look for plump ginger with thin skin. Store for 2 weeks in a dark, dry place or 1 month in an airtight bag or container in the crisper drawer in the fridge. To easily mince ginger, scrape the skin off with a small spoon and grate it with a Microplane. A 1-inch knob of ginger is about 1 tablespoon minced. For baking and roasting, use ginger powder.
Substitute: ⅛ tsp ginger powder for every fresh 1-inch knob

GLUTEN-FREE FLOUR
Favorite brand: Bob's Red Mill 1-to-1 or All-Purpose, or the homemade blend from America's Test Kitchen

GF flour mixes often use rice, buckwheat, sorghum, millet, starches, and gums to mimic gluten. If yours already contains xanthan gum, halve the recipe's amount (or omit if you're a gluten eater using all-purpose flour). Use a scale for accurate measurement, as weights vary between mixes; typically 1 cup GF flour weighs 4.2 ounces (120 grams). *Plant-based note: Check for milk powder, as it's sometimes added to encourage browning.*

GOCHUJANG
Flavor: spicy, sweet, salty, garlicky
GF brands: Sempio, Mekhala (labeled as Korean chili paste), Chung Jung One (see below)

Gochujang often contains wheat. While Chung Jung One makes theirs with rice flour—which would make it wheat-free—one of the last ingredients is seed malt, an umbrella term that could include barley. To be extra careful, try their gochujang labeled gluten-free, which still lists seed malt (rice). *Substitute: For every 1 tbsp of gochujang, use ½ tbsp GF miso paste, ½ tbsp chili paste (sambal oelek or Calabrian), and 1 tsp maple syrup.*

HONEY
Flavor: nectary, floral, fruity

When you're looking to add a sweet note to a dish, consider alternating between honey and maple syrup, as their consistency makes them easier to incorporate than sugar. Your choice might also depend on whether you're aiming for a lighter flavor (honey) or deeper flavor (maple). *Plant-based substitute: If you're vegan, substitute ¾ tsp of maple syrup for every 1 tsp of honey.*

KALAMATA OLIVES
Flavor: briny, fruity, punchy

I wasn't an olive person until I started using them to build bold flavor in my cooking. When finely chopped, they can be used as a substitute for anchovies or fermented black beans (made from soybeans), which are commonly used in Asian cooking.

KIMCHI
Flavor: spicy, tangy, funky, salty, garlicky
GF brands: Jongga, Chongga, 1st choice, Food4u, Wildbrine

Gluten-free versions of kimchi are made with rice flour or glutinous rice flour. Avoid kimchi that lists soy sauce without a breakdown of ingredients, as there may be hidden wheat flour.
Plant-based note: Check for seafood products.

LEMONS & LIMES
Flavor: bright, sour, zesty

Look for plump lemons and limes with thinner skins. Use for last-minute balance, acidity, and freshness. They typically last up to 1 month in the fridge. Always opt for freshly squeezed citrus juice instead of bottled for the best flavor.

LEMONGRASS
Flavor: citrusy, bright, herbaceous

Choose tight, plump stalks. Store in the freezer for up to 6 months and thaw for about 10 minutes before handling. Slice and remove the root plus any tough outer layers. Thinly chop from the white end until the inner purple ring disappears, and keep the green tops for infusing soups, sauces, and stews.
Substitute: 1 tsp of lemon zest for every stalk of lemongrass (it's not the same, but it'll still add a nice bright note)

MAKRUT LIME LEAVES
Flavor: citrusy, potent, bright

Crumble fresh leaves in your hand to release their fragrant aroma before adding them to dishes. Store in the freezer for up to a year.
Substitute: For every 2 fresh leaves, use 1 tsp of lime zest or 4 dried makrut lime leaves.

MAPLE SYRUP
Flavor: caramelly, sweet, earthy

I use maple syrup a lot in my cooking because its dissolvability and rich, caramelly flavor are hard to beat. It also serves as a great substitute for palm sugar, found in Southeast Asian dishes.

MIRIN
Flavor: syrupy, alcoholic, rice
GF brands: Wan Ja Shan, Mizkan, Kikkoman, Eden

An essential Japanese ingredient used in marinades, sauces, and dressings, mirin has a lower alcohol content and higher sugar content than sake. All mirin should be gluten-free in theory, but double-check the ingredients list for wheat flour, as some are not.
Substitute: A 1:1 mixture of cooking sake and maple syrup

MISO PASTE
Flavor: umami, robust, fermented
GF brands: Hanamaruki, Hikari, Shirakiku, Miko, Marukome, Kurano Kaori, Eden, Muso

White miso paste is the most likely type to be gluten-free, since it is typically made with rice. Yellow and red miso pastes may contain barley. I'm not too particular about the color, but the darker, the more intense in flavor. For a soy-free alternative, try chickpea or adzuki bean miso.

ONIONS AND SHALLOTS
Flavor: pungent, savory, sweet

Look for firm onions with smooth, delicate skins. White or yellow onions are the most versatile cooking onions. Shallots are a nice mellow alternative, while red onions pack a sharper punch. Sweet onions, like Vidalias, are the best for eating raw, as their flavor is less aggressive. Store in a dark, dry place, separate from potatoes (to prevent spoilage and sprouting), for up to 1 month.

PASTA
Flavor: mild, neutral
GF brands: Garofalo, Catelli, Jovial, Rummo, Barilla, Le Veneziane

Gluten-free pastas are getting better by the minute, with a wider range of shapes and sizes than ever before. Garofalo's penne is a reliable all-purpose pasta, while Jovial's brown rice spaghetti is best for maintaining its long shape. It's tough to find a gluten-free version of the wheat noodles used in Asian cuisines, but gluten-free spaghetti is a good replacement.

RICE (JASMINE AND SHORT-GRAIN)
Flavor: delicate, perfumed

For variety, keep smaller quantities of short-grain white and brown rice on hand; they offer a nice bite and make excellent fried rice. While steaming is the ideal reheating method (see the sidebar on page 8), you can also warm up rice and anything saucy in the microwave. Simply cover your dish with a damp paper towel and microwave for about 2 minutes (depending on your microwave's power). The damp paper towel prevents splatters and keeps food moist.

RICE NOODLES (DRIED)
Flavor: mild, neutral

While fresh rice noodles are available at some Asian supermarkets, dried ones are more reliably gluten-free and easy to store. I like to stock a range of thicknesses, from vermicelli to wide rice sticks.

RICE VINEGAR
Flavor: subtle, tangy
GF brands: Mizkan, Wan Ja Shan, Kikkoman, Marukan

Most rice vinegars are inherently gluten-free, but check for ingredients, as some also contain other grains. Rice vinegar can come seasoned or unseasoned; the former is used to make sushi rice. Get the unseasoned kind to control the amount of salt and sugar going into your dishes. *Substitutes: An equal amount of apple cider, champagne, white wine, or white balsamic vinegar*

ROASTED SESAME SEEDS
Flavor: nutty, robust, earthy

Storebought roasted sesame seeds purchased in shakers retain their flavor for up to 3 months. You can also toast your own raw seeds; see page 25. For variation in color, mix equal parts black and white sesame seeds.
Substitutes: An equal amount of white or black poppy seeds or finely chopped nuts (depending on the application)

SALT
Flavor: sharp, briny

The most essential flavor enhancer in my kitchen is Diamond Crystal kosher salt. I learned to love it during my time in restaurants, so using it has become second nature. Its coarse but not-too-coarse grains make it ideal for sprinkling with your fingers, the perfect touch to any dish.
Substitutes: ½ the amount of table salt or fine sea salt

SCALLIONS
Flavor: oniony, delicate, grassy

Look for skinnier scallions, firm to the touch with a vibrant green color. Store in a damp paper towel in a storage bag in the fridge for up to 2 weeks. Give any unused scallion whites new life by putting the roots in a glass with about 2 inches of water. Place by a sunny window and they'll regrow in a week!
Substitute: An equal amount of ramps or chives

SOY SAUCE OR TAMARI
Flavor: salty, umami, caramelly
GF brands: Kikkoman, Lee Kum Kee, Wan Ja Shan, Yamasa, Bragg, San-J, Ichibiki, Datu Puti

Soy sauce and tamari can be used interchangeably, although tamari has a more intense flavor. The main difference is that soy sauce often contains wheat, while tamari is usually made with fermented rice (koji). That said, always double-check a tamari's ingredients, as some not labeled as gluten-free might still contain wheat. Coconut aminos is a soy-free alternative with a sweeter taste and is always gluten-free.
Substitutes: An equal amount of coconut aminos or fish sauce

STOCK (VEGETABLE, CHICKEN, BEEF)
Flavor: savory, rich, mellow

An indispensable ingredient for building flavor in soups, sauces, and stews. I have a convenient homemade recipe on page 24, but if you're using store-bought stock, check for gluten-containing ingredients like barley extract.
Substitutes: 1 tsp of GF miso paste or bouillon paste per 1 cup of water, adjusting the salt in the recipe to taste

TAHINI
Flavor: sesame, creamy, rich

Tahini is a natural choice in Asian cooking because of the continent's abundance of sesame. For a thinner and, to me, more desirable consistency, store at room temperature instead of in the fridge, just like other nut and seed butters.
Substitute: Natural peanut, almond, or cashew butter: ¾ the amount, plus a splash of water to thin it out

TOASTED SESAME OIL
Flavor: nutty, robust, earthy
Favorite brand: Kadoya

Unlike sesame oil made from raw sesame seeds, the toasted variety is more of a flavoring oil than a cooking oil, and a little goes a long way. Kadoya's toasted sesame oil is extra concentrated in flavor and widely available. Store in the fridge.

TOMATO PASTE
Flavor: savory, tart, sweet
Favorite brand: Mutti

When it comes to tomato paste, the squeezable tube is where it's at! It's a convenient way to enhance and round out the flavors of a dish.

BUILDING BLOCKS

These essential recipes are the heart and soul of my cooking: simple techniques are paired with flavor-boosting wonders for everything from stocks to sauces. They're called building blocks for a reason! So simple but so important, each adds layers of complexity to a dish without making the recipes overly complicated. Freezer Bag Stock (page 24) is an easy, waste-free way to use food scraps to make a recipe staple, and you probably already have everything in your pantry for the game-changing Flavor Bomb Dressing (page 27).

While each side, dressing, sauce, and staple is paired with at least one dish in the book (for instance, the Chili Miso Sauce makes the 'Shroom Toast on page 132 sing), the best part about this chapter is that these recipes can be used with all sorts of dishes beyond these pages. Level up any salad with the Ponzu Maple Vinaigrette (page 28), and brighten up any meal with the quick and satisfying Simple Dressed Greens (page 25). My ultimate goal is to inspire more ease and adventurousness in your kitchen!

So take these quick pickles and punchy vinaigrettes and make them your own. Discover how different flavors and techniques can seamlessly come together in unexpected ways—especially if you have specific dietary needs. There's even a formula to help you master your own flavorful dressings without a recipe. Use the recipes as a starting point, and let your creativity run wild!

ESSENTIALS

FREEZER BAG STOCK

MAKES ABOUT 12 TO 16 CUPS

Vegetable scraps, such as mushroom stems, carrot peels, onion skins, garlic skins, cilantro stems, scallion whites, celery ends, corn cobs, tomato ends, and/or daikon peels

Protein scraps, as needed for specific kinds of stock: chicken bones, pork bones, or shellfish shells

Optional additions: kombu, dried shiitake mushrooms, ginger slices, lemongrass ends

10 to 12 cups water

NOTE In a pinch, when a recipe calls for stock, you can use 1 teaspoon of GF bouillon or miso paste for every 1 cup of water. Adjust the amount of salt in the recipe to taste.

1. Fill a large freezer bag with food scraps until full. Freeze for up to 3 months.

2. Place the food scraps in a large stock pot and cover with water. Bring to a boil. Reduce the heat to low, cover, and simmer for 1 hour.

3. Using a colander, strain the stock into a large bowl and let cool.

4. Store in a few quart-sized deli containers in the fridge for up to 5 days or in the freezer for up to 3 months.

STEAMED RICE: STOVETOP METHOD

SERVES 3 TO 4 (ABOUT 3 CUPS)

1 cup jasmine or short-grain white rice

1¼ cups water

A pinch of kosher salt

A drizzle of neutral oil

1. Using a strainer, rinse the rice until the water runs clear. Transfer the rice to a medium saucepan and add the water and the salt and oil.

2. Bring the rice to a simmer on medium heat. Reduce the heat to low, cover, and simmer for 18 minutes or until the liquid is absorbed and the rice is tender. Turn off the heat and let it sit on the element for 5 minutes. Fluff the rice with a paddle or fork before serving.

STEAMED RICE: RICE COOKER METHOD

SERVES 2 TO 3 (ABOUT 2¼ CUPS)

1 rice cooker cup (equivalent to ¾ cup) jasmine or short-grain white rice

A pinch of kosher salt

NOTE For the sake of easy math, these steamed rice methods are designed to yield different quantities. Don't worry about having too much rice, as leftovers are perfect for creating delicious fried rice with my formula (page 136). Store any excess rice in an airtight container or storage bag in the fridge for up to 5 days.

1. Rinse and swirl the rice in the rice cooker bowl. Pour out the water and repeat until the water runs clear. Add enough water to just reach the 1 cup line on the rice cooker bowl and add the salt.

2. Turn the machine on and, if your rice cooker gives the option, set it to the Plain or White Rice setting. The rice cooker will switch to the Keep Warm setting once it's done cooking. Fluff the rice with a paddle or fork before serving.

TOASTED NUTS OR SEEDS

1 cup raw whole nuts or seeds, like peanuts, walnuts, hazelnuts, macadamias, pecans, pistachios, pine nuts, pumpkin seeds, sesame seeds, sunflower seeds, cashews, or almonds

1. In a large frying pan, toast the nuts or seeds on medium heat for 3 to 4 minutes, until fragrant and golden, tossing frequently. Transfer the nuts or seeds to a plate and set aside to cool, about 5 to 10 minutes.

2. Store in an airtight container for up to 1 month.

BRIGHT SIDES

SIMPLE DRESSED GREENS

SERVES 1

A few handfuls of tender mixed greens

A drizzle of toasted sesame oil

A drizzle of rice vinegar

Kosher salt to taste

1. In a bowl, using clean hands, salad servers, or tongs, lightly toss together the greens, sesame oil, rice vinegar and salt.

PICKLED RED ONIONS OR VEG

MAKES ABOUT 2 CUPS

16 oz (500 ml) mason jar

1 red onion, thinly sliced, or 2 carrots, julienned, or ½ small daikon, julienned

½ cup boiling-hot water

½ cup white vinegar

¼ cup granulated sugar

1. In the mason jar, combine the vegetables, hot water, vinegar, and sugar. Close tightly with the lid and shake to dissolve the sugar. Place in the fridge. Red onion pickles will be ready in as soon as 1 hour, but overnight is best for all of the vegetable options.

2. Store in an airtight container in the fridge for up to 2 weeks.

QUICK PICKLED RED ONIONS OR SHALLOTS

MAKES ABOUT 1 CUP

½ red onion, or 2 small shallots, thinly sliced

2 tbsp lime juice

1 tsp granulated sugar

½ tsp kosher salt

NOTE Turn to this recipe when time is short, but you crave the brightness of pickled red onions or shallots.

1. In a medium bowl, combine the onions, lime juice, sugar, and salt. Massage the onions lightly with your hands. Let sit for 30 minutes to 1 hour before using.

DRESSING FORMULA

This simple dressing formula makes it a breeze to whip up and play with different flavor combinations. I recommend making larger batches with shelf-stable ingredients in a mason jar or squeeze bottle, for effortless salads in no time. Dressings can be stored in the fridge for up to 2 weeks unless they contain fresh ingredients (including citrus juice), in which case they should be used within 5 days.

START WITH BOTH

ACID (1 part) to cut through the oil and make it pop! This could be:

- Vinegar, like rice, cider, white wine, red wine, balsamic, Chinese black, white distilled, champagne, or sherry
- Citrus juice, like grapefruit, orange, lemon, lime, or yuzu

AND

EMULSIFIER (1 part) to unify the dressing to help it cling to salad ingredients! This could be:

- Mustard, like hot, Dijon, yellow, or grainy
- Mayonnaise (which has a natural emulsifier in egg yolks)
- Yogurt (which has a natural emulsifier in milk proteins)

FLAVOR IT WITH

SALT (to taste, about ⅛ tsp per ¼ cup of dressing) to pull out natural flavors! Learn to use:

- Kosher salt, the best all-purpose salt, as anyone who has ever worked in a restaurant knows; the larger salt crystals are more tactile than table salt, making it easy to learn quantities by sight and touch

YOU CAN ALSO ADD

SOMETHING SWEET (to taste, about ½ tsp per ¼ cup dressing), to round out sharp flavors! Sweeteners also aid in emulsifying. This could be:

- Liquid honey, maple syrup, agave nectar, or jam (which all dissolve easily at room temperature)

AN UMAMI BOMB (a dash):

- GF soy sauce, tamari, or miso paste, minced anchovies, shrimp paste, or fish sauce

AND/ OR

YOUR FAVORITE SEASONINGS (a dash)—you can get creative here, using anything, like:

- Black pepper, ground spices, dried herbs, capers, chopped olives, chili oil or paste, tahini, nut butter, nut oil, or sesame oil

FRESH INGREDIENTS (to taste), like any of the following:

- Chopped hearty herbs or minced garlic, shallots, ginger, or fresh chilies

THEN SLOWLY WHISK IN

HEALTHY OIL (3 parts), as the bulk of the dressing. This could be:

- Sunflower, safflower, or grapeseed oil (all high in vitamin E), extra virgin olive oil, or avocado oil (high in healthy monounsaturated fats)

DRESSINGS

A note on shelf life: any dressing containing fresh ingredients (citrus juice, fresh herbs, garlic, etc.) is best used within 5 days, while those with only shelf-stable ingredients can be used for up to 2 weeks.

FLAVOR BOMB DRESSING
MAKES ABOUT ½ CUP

1 small shallot, minced (about 2 tbsp)

1 cup boiling-hot water

½ tbsp freshly cracked black pepper

3 tbsp extra virgin olive oil

2 tbsp GF soy sauce or tamari

1½ tbsp rice vinegar

1 tbsp toasted sesame oil

½ tbsp mirin, or 1 tsp unsalted cooking sake
  + ½ tsp maple syrup

½ tbsp Dijon mustard

1. In a medium bowl, soak the minced shallots in the hot water for 5 minutes. Drain with a fine-mesh strainer.

2. Using an immersion blender in a tall cup or a small stand blender, blend the shallots, pepper, olive oil, soy sauce, rice vinegar, sesame oil, mirin, and mustard until uniform in consistency.

3. Store in an airtight container in the fridge for up to 5 days.

FRIED SHALLOT DRESSING
MAKES ABOUT ½ CUP

1 tbsp GF fried shallots

¼ cup extra virgin olive oil

2 tbsp GF soy sauce, tamari, or fish sauce

1½ tbsp rice vinegar

1 tbsp Dijon or grainy mustard

½ tbsp maple syrup

1. Using an immersion blender in a tall cup or a small stand blender, blend the shallots, olive oil, soy sauce, rice vinegar, mustard, and maple syrup until uniform in consistency.

2. Store in an airtight container in the fridge for up to 5 days.

NOTE When dressing your salad with Fried Shallot Dressing, garnish it with additional fried shallots!

LEMON GINGER VINAIGRETTE
MAKES ABOUT ½ CUP

1-inch knob ginger, minced

2 tbsp lemon juice

1 tbsp grainy mustard

1 tbsp maple syrup

1 tsp toasted sesame oil

½ tsp chili paste (such as sambal oelek or Calabrian)

¼ cup extra virgin olive oil

1. In a medium bowl, combine the ginger, lemon juice, mustard, maple syrup, sesame oil, and chili paste. Slowly whisk in the olive oil until emulsified.

2. Store in an airtight container in the fridge for up to 5 days.

MISO TAHINI DRESSING

MAKES ABOUT ⅓ CUP

2 tbsp rice vinegar

1 tbsp room-temperature tahini

1 tbsp GF miso paste

½ tbsp maple syrup

1 tsp chili oil (such as chili crisp)

1. In a medium bowl, whisk together the rice vinegar, tahini, miso, maple syrup, chili oil, and a splash of water until uniform in consistency.

2. Store in an airtight container in the fridge for up to 2 weeks.

NUOC CHAM VINAIGRETTE

MAKES ABOUT ⅓ CUP

1 tbsp lime juice (about ½ lime)

1 tbsp maple syrup

½ tbsp GF fish sauce, soy sauce, or tamari

1 tsp toasted sesame oil

1 tsp grainy or Dijon mustard

2 tbsp extra virgin olive oil

1. In a small bowl, combine the lime juice, maple syrup, fish sauce, sesame oil, and mustard. Slowly whisk in the olive oil until emulsified.

2. Store in an airtight container in the fridge for up to 5 days.

PONZU MAPLE VINAIGRETTE

MAKES ABOUT ⅔ CUP

½ small shallot, finely minced (about 1 tbsp) (optional)

2 tbsp GF soy sauce or tamari

2 tbsp lemon, lime, or yuzu juice

1 tbsp Dijon or grainy mustard

2 tsp maple syrup, or 1½ tsp liquid honey

¼ cup extra virgin olive oil

1. In a small bowl, whisk together the shallot (if using), soy sauce, lemon juice, mustard, and maple syrup. Slowly whisk in the olive oil until emulsified.

2. Store in an airtight container in the fridge for up to 5 days (with shallots) or up to 2 weeks (without shallots).

SILKEN TOFU CAESAR DRESSING

MAKES ABOUT 2 CUPS

14 oz (400 g) silken tofu

2 cloves garlic, sliced

½ ripe avocado

½ tsp freshly cracked black pepper

¼ tsp kosher salt

2 tbsp extra virgin olive oil

1 tbsp lime juice

1 tbsp rice vinegar

1 tbsp GF fermented black beans (see note)

½ tbsp GF soy sauce or tamari

½ tbsp maple syrup

½ tbsp toasted sesame oil

½ tsp chili paste (such as sambal oelek or Calabrian)

1. Using an immersion blender in a tall cup or a small stand blender, blend the tofu, garlic, avocado, pepper, salt, olive oil, lime juice, rice vinegar, fermented black beans, soy sauce, maple syrup, sesame oil, and chili paste until uniform in consistency.

2. Store in an airtight container in the fridge for up to 3 days.

NOTE If you can't find gluten-free fermented black beans, which are actually fermented soybeans, use chopped pitted kalamata olives.

SAUCES

CHILI MISO SAUCE
MAKES ABOUT ½ CUP

1 tbsp roasted sesame seeds

1 tsp garlic powder

½ tsp unsalted Korean chili flakes (gochugaru) or Kashmiri chili powder

2 tbsp GF miso paste

1 tbsp lime or lemon juice

1 tbsp GF soy sauce or tamari

1 tbsp maple syrup

1 tsp toasted sesame oil

1 tsp water

1. In a small bowl, whisk together the sesame seeds, garlic powder, chili flakes, miso, lime juice, soy sauce, maple syrup, water, and sesame oil until uniform in consistency.

2. Store in an airtight container in the fridge for up to 5 days.

SUB
If you can't find gochugaru or Kashmiri chili powder, use ½ tsp mild paprika + ⅛ tsp cayenne.

DUMPLING SAUCE
MAKES ABOUT ¼ CUP

2 tbsp GF soy sauce or tamari

1 tbsp GF Chinese black vinegar (or see page 13 for sub)

1 tbsp chili paste (such as sambal oelek or Calabrian)

½ tbsp toasted sesame oil

1. In a small bowl, whisk together the soy sauce, vinegar, chili paste, and sesame oil.

2. Store in an airtight container in the fridge for up to 2 weeks.

NUOC CHAM
MAKES ABOUT ⅓ CUP

2 tbsp lime juice (about 1 lime)

2 tbsp maple syrup

1 tbsp GF fish sauce

1 clove garlic, minced (optional)

½ long red Thai chili, minced, or 1 tsp chili paste (such as sambal oelek or Calabrian)

1. In a small bowl, whisk together the lime juice, maple syrup, fish sauce, garlic (if using), and chili.

2. Store in an airtight container in the fridge for up to 5 days.

LEMONY NUOC CHAM
MAKES ABOUT ⅓ CUP

2 tbsp lemon juice

2 tbsp maple syrup

1 tbsp GF fish sauce, soy sauce, or tamari

1. In a small bowl, whisk together the lemon juice, maple syrup, and fish sauce.

2. Store in an airtight container in the fridge for up to 5 days.

SCALLION GINGER OIL
MAKES ABOUT 1 CUP

4 tbsp neutral high-heat cooking oil

8 scallions, chopped

2-inch knob ginger, minced

½ tsp kosher salt

1. In a small nonstick frying pan, heat the oil on medium heat until it shimmers, about 1 to 2 minutes. (Never walk away from hot oil, as it can catch on fire.) Turn off the heat.

2. Add the scallions, ginger, and salt to the pan, stirring as it sizzles with a silicone spatula or a wooden spoon. Set aside to cool completely.

3. Store in an airtight container in the fridge for up to 5 days.

SESAME CHILI MAYO
MAKES ABOUT ½ CUP

½ cup mayonnaise

2 tsp toasted sesame oil

2 tsp chili paste (such as sambal oelek or Calabrian)

1. In a small bowl, whisk together the mayonnaise, sesame oil, and chili paste.

2. Store in an airtight container in the fridge for up to 2 weeks.

SSAMJANG
MAKES ABOUT ¾ CUP

¼ cup GF miso paste

¼ cup water

2 tbsp toasted sesame oil

2 tbsp GF gochujang (Korean chili paste), or 1 tbsp GF miso paste, 1 tbsp chili paste (such as sambal oelek or Calabrian), and 1 tsp maple syrup

2 tsp roasted sesame seeds

2 tsp maple syrup

1. In a small bowl, whisk together the miso, water, sesame oil, gochujang, sesame seeds, and maple syrup until uniform in consistency.

2. Store in an airtight container in the fridge for up to 2 weeks.

THAI BASIL PESTO

MAKES ABOUT 1 CUP

1 clove garlic, sliced

1 cup fresh Thai basil, roughly chopped

1 cup fresh cilantro, roughly chopped

¼ cup toasted peanuts (see page 25)

½ tsp kosher salt

6 tbsp extra virgin olive oil

1 tbsp lime juice (about ½ lime)

1. In a blender or food processor, combine the garlic, basil, cilantro, peanuts, salt, olive oil, and lime juice. Blitz to combine. (Or, if you have a mortar and pestle, pound the first five ingredients into a paste, then mix with the oil and lime juice in a bowl.)

2. Store in an airtight container in the fridge for up to 5 days.

PANDAN KAYA

MAKES ABOUT 2½ CUPS

4 full pandan leaves (see note)

1 cup coconut milk

1 cup granulated sugar

5 large eggs

A pinch of kosher salt

NOTE

Try pandan kaya as a replacement for syrup on my Pandan Kaya French Toast (page 229), Cornmeal Mochi Pancakes (page 206), or Coconut Mochi Waffles (page 209). Pandan leaves can be found fresh or frozen at your local East or Southeast Asian supermarket.

1. Using scissors, snip the pandan leaves into 2-inch pieces.

2. In a blender, blend the pandan leaves with the coconut milk until the leaves have broken down into tiny pieces. Using a sieve, strain out the fibrous leaves, leaving behind a light-green-tinted coconut milk.

3. In a medium saucepan, whisk together the pandan-infused coconut milk and sugar. Heat on medium heat until the sugar has dissolved and the liquid is steaming. Remove from the heat.

4. In a medium bowl, whisk the eggs until uniform in color. Place a damp rag under the bowl to keep it from wobbling and slowly pour in a steady stream of pandan milk to temper the eggs, whisking briskly until it is all combined.

5. Fill a large bowl halfway with an ice bath. Return the pandan milk to the saucepan and cook on medium heat, whisking constantly, for 3 to 5 minutes, until just thickened. You are looking for a light, pudding-like consistency. Season with salt.

6. Immediately place the saucepan in the ice bath so the custard will cool quickly. Keep whisking until the custard is cool to touch.

7. For an extra-smooth custard, blend with an immersion or stand blender, or pass through a sieve.

8. Transfer the custard to mason jars and refrigerate for up to 2 weeks.

TOSSED
AND ASSEMBLED

The ability to make a great salad is a true test of a good cook. It requires using your intuition by tasting as you go, and highlighting the best possible ingredients with a balance of salty, acidic, sweet, and texturally satisfying components. It involves adapting simple techniques to what's available and appealing, building confidence in creating without a recipe. I've carried this lesson forward: modifying dishes to suit whatever current limitations I'm faced with has allowed me to create exciting food without compromise, regardless of the dietary restrictions that come my way.

Taste, taste, taste, and go with your gut! Too acidic? Add a bit of sweetener. Have sweet potatoes lying around? Roast them up and toss them in your salad. Want to keep things exciting? Add unexpected chili oil to your dressing. Make the recipes work for *you*, not the other way around (this coming from a reluctant recipe follower who can't *just* make a box of macaroni and cheese without adding a personal touch). This approach has led to delightful surprises, such as when I added leftover Dumpling Sauce to Peak Summer Salad with Burrata (page 43) and leftover Scallion Ginger Oil to Tomatoes with Feta (page 35).

Over the years, I've blended this practice with my love of Asian flavors, creating salads that are colorful, texturally satisfying, and straightforward to assemble, while highlighting ingredients at their prime. I love a big ol' platter of salad as a radiant centerpiece to show that veg can be super exciting!

The recipes in this chapter are fresh, vibrant, and adaptable, with minimal cooking involved. They pair well with the more decadent dishes found in the Fried & Sizzled (page 129) and Grilled & Roasted (page 167) chapters.

Scan me to listen along!

TOMATOES WITH FETA & SCALLION GINGER OIL

Inspired by Caprese salad and Cantonese BBQ shops

♫ *Agitations tropicales – L'Impératrice*

SERVES 2 TO 4

Scallion ginger oil is a condiment typically served at bustling Cantonese BBQ restaurants alongside a showcase of succulent roasted meats. I love its ability to amp up the flavor in various dishes, like in my Silken Tofu Salad with Tamari & Scallion Ginger Oil (page 44) and this straightforward tomato dish. This is what happens when Caprese salad meets the familiar Chinese flavors I grew up eating—a manifestation of my curiosity to experiment with tastes influenced by growing up in Canada.

2 beefsteak or heirloom tomatoes, sliced into rounds

½ recipe Scallion Ginger Oil (page 30)

A drizzle of extra virgin olive oil

A drizzle of GF Chinese black vinegar (or see page 13 for sub)

2 tbsp crumbled feta cheese

Kosher salt and freshly cracked black pepper to taste

DAIRY-FREE/PLANT-BASED OPTION

Feta → 6 pitted green olives (Castelvetrano), roughly chopped

1. Lay out the tomato slices on a serving plate. Using a spoon, dollop the scallion ginger oil over top. Lightly drizzle with olive oil and vinegar. Garnish with the feta. Season with salt and pepper.

ORANGE & ASIAN PEAR SLAW

with Lemony Nuoc Cham

SERVES 4 🥢 ☘ 🌿

Inspired by Vietnamese jicama salads

♫ *Mornin Dew – Sunni Colón*

My love language is fresh-cut fruit, naturally—I'm a kid of Chinese immigrants. What's better than a plate of ready-to-eat, perfectly ripe fruit that captures the vitality of life itself? In the depths of winter, I like to liven things up with this energizing slaw that harnesses the brightness of sunny oranges and sweet Asian pears. Green cabbage acts as a neutral, crunchy base, allowing the floral herbs and tangy dressing to bring out the natural sweetness of the fruit. For an assortment of lively colors, use different varieties of oranges, such as blood, cara caras, and the universal navels.

½ green cabbage (10½ oz/300 g), finely shredded

2 Asian pears, peeled and cut into thick batons

2 oranges, peeled and segmented

2 sprigs fresh mint, chopped

2 sprigs fresh dill, chopped

Lemony Nuoc Cham (page 30)

¼ cup toasted peanuts (see page 25), roughly chopped

¼ cup GF fried shallots

A drizzle of extra virgin olive oil

Kosher salt to taste

PLANT-BASED OPTION
Use GF soy sauce or tamari in the nuoc cham

SUB
For those with peanut allergies, substitute other toasted nuts, pumpkin seeds, or sunflower seeds.

1. In a large bowl, combine the cabbage, pears, oranges, mint, and dill. Pour the nuoc cham over top and gently mix with tongs or salad servers. Garnish with the peanuts and shallots. Lightly drizzle olive oil over top and season with salt.

FLAVOR BOMB EDAMAME

SERVES 6 TO 8

This finger-licking good edamame draws inspo from my time working at a Vietnamese restaurant in Montreal. It was at HÀ that my passion for Asian flavors was reignited, following a few years in traditional French kitchens at the start of my culinary journey. The restaurant served as a vibrant microcosm of Asian-Canadian culture, with its boldly flavored cuisine and unforgettable French kitchen lingo echoing throughout the kitchen: "en commande," "une soupe coco!" "OUI, CHEF!"

1 package (17.6 oz/500 g) frozen edamame in pods

Flavor Bomb Dressing (page 27) to taste

2 tbsp roasted sesame seeds

Fresh cilantro, chopped (optional)

½ lime, cut into wedges

1. Bring a medium pot of salted water to a boil on high heat. Add the edamame and blanch for 5 minutes. Drain in a strainer or colander.

2. Transfer the edamame to a large bowl and toss with a few tablespoons of the flavor bomb dressing. Garnish with the sesame seeds and cilantro (if using). Serve with lime wedges.

HERBACEOUS MELON SALAD

with Bacon & Nuoc Cham Vinaigrette

Inspired by
prosciutto-wrapped melon
♫ *How Long Do I Have to
Wait for You?*
– Sharon Jones & the Dap-Kings

SERVES 4

My family instilled in me a deep appreciation for fruit from an early age, and I will always find ways to highlight whatever fruit is in season. This recipe combines juicy and nectary cantaloupe with leafy greens, aromatic herbs, salty bacon bits, and a trusted gluten-free fish-lime vinaigrette for an indulgent and feel-good salad, 'cause I'm all about that balance.

4 slices bacon

4 large handfuls of tender leafy lettuce (such as mâche, Bibb, oak leaf, or any baby lettuce), torn into bite-sized pieces

½ English cucumber, seeded and sliced into crescents

1 cup snow peas or sugar snap peas, strings removed, halved on a diagonal

8 sprigs fresh mint, basil (Thai or Italian), dill, and/or cilantro, chopped

¼ ripe cantaloupe, honeydew, or watermelon, cubed

2 tbsp Nuoc Cham Vinaigrette (page 28), plus more to taste

Kosher salt and freshly cracked black pepper to taste

PLANT-BASED/PESCATARIAN OPTION

• Bacon bits → ¼ cup GF fried shallots

• Use GF soy sauce or tamari in the vinaigrette

1. In a medium nonstick frying pan, fry the bacon on medium-low heat until just crispy, about 8 to 10 minutes, flipping frequently. Transfer to a plate lined with a paper towel to absorb grease. On a cutting board, chop the bacon into bite-sized bits.

2. In a large bowl, combine the lettuce, cucumbers, peas, herbs, and melon. Dress the salad with the vinaigrette and gently mix with tongs or salad servers, adding more vinaigrette to taste. Garnish with the bacon bits. Season with salt and pepper.

NOTES

Pick melons with a sweet, melony aroma. If they don't have much scent at the store, you can ripen one on your kitchen counter for a few days until it does.

Dispose of any excess bacon fat in a clean, empty can and store it in the fridge until it's full enough to throw out.

Blend any leftover melon with ice and a dash of sugar for a refreshing summer drink.

PEAK SUMMER SALAD

with Burrata & Dumpling Sauce

SERVES 4 TO 6

Inspired by the restaurant Reyna

♫ *Le temps est bon*
– Bon Entendeur and Isabelle Pierre

This dish is an homage to a Filipino restaurant in Paris called Reyna, where Reid and I devoured a burrata dish that came bathing in a pool of chili scallion ginger oil—pure joie de vivre, as they say in France. I wanted to recapture the feeling we got from eating that dish with my favorite peak summer crops—sunny garden tomatoes, refreshing cukes, and Niagara peaches that are so damn juicy you need to eat them over the sink. Dress it all with my go-to dumpling sauce and some hunkin', luscious burrata, and you have joy on a plate, baby! The way the chefs at restaurants like Reyna fuse flavors inspires me to push the boundaries of what my cooking can be, especially considering the criticism that chefs of color often face for not being "authentic," which limits our ability to create outside the box. I firmly believe that when we recognize and learn about a dish's origins, food can be a powerful expression of personal experience.

2 freestone peaches, sliced into wedges

2 beefsteak or heirloom tomatoes, cored and sliced into wedges

½ English cucumber, halved lengthwise and sliced into half moons

Dumpling Sauce (page 29)

1 ball (8 oz/225 g) fresh burrata cheese (see note)

A drizzle of extra virgin olive oil

GARNISHES

Fresh cilantro and/or basil (Thai or Italian), chopped

1 tbsp roasted white sesame seeds

1 tbsp GF fried garlic or shallots

1 tsp chili oil (such as chili crisp)

Fresh edible flowers, for garnish (optional)

DAIRY-FREE/PLANT-BASED OPTION

Burrata → soft or silken tofu

1. In a large bowl, combine the peaches, tomatoes, and cucumbers. Toss with half of the dumpling sauce. Using a slotted spoon, transfer the salad to a large platter, leaving behind any liquid to discard.

2. With the same slotted spoon, make a crater in the center of the salad and nestle the burrata inside. Lightly drizzle olive oil and the remaining dumpling sauce over top. Sprinkle with the garnishes. Using a small paring knife, cut the burrata into four to six pieces.

NOTES

If burrata is hard to find, substitute with fresh mozzarella or bocconcini.

SILKEN TOFU SALAD

with Tamari & Scallion Ginger Oil

Inspired by hot summer days

♫ *Ondulation*
– Burning Peacocks

SERVES 2 TO 4

Gluten-free peeps, enter the realm of delightfully dressed silken tofu! Most versions at restaurants are served with soy sauce dressings that contain gluten. Echoing the texture of panna cotta, this chilled tofu features plump cherry tomatoes for explosions of tart with sweet, crisp cucumbers, and flavor-packed scallion ginger oil for a truly refreshing snack.

½ cup cherry tomatoes, halved

1 mini cucumber, sliced into half moons

1 tbsp rice vinegar

1 tbsp GF soy sauce or tamari

1 tbsp maple syrup

10½ oz (300 g) silken or soft tofu, drained and sliced into ⅜-inch-thick rectangles

½ recipe Scallion Ginger Oil (page 30)

GARNISHES

2 tbsp GF fried shallots

1 tsp roasted sesame seeds

GF chili oil (such as chili crisp) (optional)

Fresh or dried edible flowers (optional)

Kosher salt to taste

1. In a medium bowl, combine the tomatoes, cucumbers, rice vinegar, soy sauce, and maple syrup.

2. On a serving plate, fan out the tofu slices on top of each other like fallen dominoes. Using a spoon, arrange the dressed cherry tomatoes and cucumbers around the tofu. Dollop scallion ginger oil over top. Sprinkle with the garnishes, finishing with salt.

NOTE
Silken or soft tofu can be found at your local Asian grocery store.

COCONUT LIME CEVICHE WITH GOLDEN KIWI

Inspired by Filipino kinilaw

♫ *Sun Models (feat. Madelyn Grant)* – ODESZA

SERVES 2 TO 4 🥄 🌿

While ceviche may seem intimidating to make at home, it's surprisingly easy once you've sourced the freshest fish you can get your hands on. It's a good chance to master the art of balancing salt, fat, and acid—the first three fundamentals of good cooking, according to Samin Nosrat. This ceviche, inspired by Filipino kinilaw, is made with lime juice and beautifully balanced with bright makrut lime leaves, rich coconut milk, and pops of sweetness from the golden kiwi. It's a restaurant-quality dish without the common worry of gluten contamination in the fried shallots and corn chips served alongside it.

4 tbsp full-fat coconut milk

1-inch knob ginger, minced

2 makrut lime leaves, stem removed, finely chopped, or 1 tsp lime zest

12 oz (340 g) high-quality skinless white fish fillets (such as bass, rockfish, red snapper, grouper, albacore tuna, mahi mahi, or halibut), cut into ½-inch cubes

1 small shallot, thinly sliced (about 2 tbsp)

2 tbsp lime juice (about 1 lime), plus more as needed

1 tsp kosher salt, plus more as needed

2 golden kiwis, cubed (about ⅓ cup)

1 long red Thai chili, thinly sliced, or a drizzle of GF chili oil (such as chili crisp)

2 tbsp GF fried shallots

Fresh cilantro and/or basil (Thai or Italian), chopped

A drizzle of extra virgin olive oil

2 large handfuls of GF corn tortilla chips

½ lime, cut into wedges

1. In a small bowl, combine the coconut milk, ginger, and lime leaves. Set aside.

2. In another small bowl, combine the fish, shallots, lime juice, and salt. Using a spoon, toss to cure until the outer layer of the fish is white, about 1 minute.

3. Mix the cured fish with the coconut milk mixture. Adjust the salt and lime juice to taste.

4. Plate the ceviche and top with the kiwis, chilies, fried shallots, and herbs. Drizzle with olive oil. Serve immediately with the corn chips and lime wedges.

NOTE

If you can't find golden kiwis, you can substitute with yellow mangoes. I wouldn't recommend using green kiwis, as I find them too acidic for this dish.

TUNA & CURRY-ROASTED CHICKPEA SALAD

with Ponzu Maple Vinaigrette

Inspired by Japanese
bottled dressings

♫ *Going Straight Crazy (feat. Princess
Shaw) – Galactic*

SERVES 4 🥄 🌱 🍃

I love savory Japanese salad dressings, but stores don't usually sell gluten-free versions. That's why the Ponzu Maple Vinaigrette (page 28) has become a reliable option in our home. Combined with canned tuna in olive oil, curry-roasted chickpeas, and luscious avocado, it makes for a light and nutritious meal. If you can find yuzu juice at a Japanese market, definitely indulge and use it in the dressing, as it will truly elevate this salad!

1 can (14 oz/398 ml) chickpeas, rinsed and drained (about 1½ cups)

1 tbsp curry powder

½ tsp kosher salt, plus more to taste

1 tbsp neutral high-heat cooking oil

2 romaine hearts, ends removed, chopped

1 can (6 oz/170 g) tuna in olive oil, drained

1 beefsteak or heirloom tomato, cored and sliced into wedges

½ English cucumber, halved lengthwise and sliced into half moons

4 scallions, green parts only, chopped

1 large avocado, diced

Ponzu Maple Vinaigrette (page 28) to taste

Freshly cracked black pepper to taste

PLANT-BASED OPTION

Omit canned tuna

1. Preheat the oven or toaster oven to 400°F (200°C). Line a baking sheet with parchment paper or foil.

2. In a large bowl, toss the chickpeas, curry powder, salt, and oil to combine. Spread out in a single layer on the prepared pan. Roast for 20 minutes, tossing halfway through, until crispy and golden.

3. In a large bowl, combine the romaine, tuna, tomatoes, cucumbers, scallions, avocados, and chickpeas. Dress with a few tablespoons of the vinaigrette and gently toss with tongs or salad servers. Season with salt and pepper.

NOTES

For a deluxe version, substitute the canned tuna with my Sesame Tuna Steaks with Ponzu (page 190).

CRISP CABBAGE SLAW

SERVES 4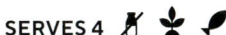

Inspired by
J. Kenji López-Alt's coleslaw

♫ *Tormenta (feat. Bad Bunny)*
– Gorillaz

Never have wet, soggy slaw again! This is our go-to crispy slaw that embodies the balance and versatility of this book. It instantly brightens any meal and goes well with just about any dressing. I love it with Nuoc Cham Vinaigrette (page 28), but seriously, try it with any dressing from the Building Blocks chapter. Following Kenji's advice, the trick is to draw out as much moisture as possible with a combination of sugar and salt, plus a quick spin in a salad spinner, guaranteeing crisp and flavorful veggies every time! Serve it as a side or use it as a base with your fave protein.

¼ small red cabbage, thinly sliced

¼ small green cabbage, thinly sliced

1 carrot, julienned

1 red bell pepper, julienned

1½ tbsp granulated sugar

1 tsp kosher salt

Fresh cilantro, basil (Thai or Italian), mint, or dill, chopped (optional)

Dressing of choice (pages 26–28)

1. In a large bowl, combine the red cabbage, green cabbage, carrot, and red pepper. Sprinkle with the sugar and salt. Using your hands, very gently massage the sugar and salt into the vegetables until well mixed and dissolved. Let sit for 15 minutes.

2. In a salad spinner, spin the vegetables until most of the liquid has released. (It will be more than you ever imagined.)

3. Dress the slaw with the herbs (if using) and your dressing of choice and gently toss with tongs or salad servers.

4. Store in an airtight container in the fridge for up to 1 week.

NOTES

A salad spinner is essential for crisp and crunchy slaw (and all salads, for that matter).

Feel free to double or triple this recipe at the beginning of the week, but hold off on adding the herbs until serving, as they'll wilt quickly.

If you feel like going all in on carrots, you can swap out the bell pepper for another carrot. Other great last-minute additions include napa cabbage, mango, and pomelo.

CHARRED CORN SALAD
with Coconut Cream

SERVES 4 🌶 🌱 🍃

Inspired by Thai street corn

♫ *Cocoon – Milky Chance*

Nothing says late summer like farm-fresh corn, golden and charred on a grill. When I find myself with leftover grilled corn cobs, I make this salad with crunchy bell peppers, sharp red onions, spicy jalapeños, and an abundance of herbs—they just make any dish taste so fresh! If you can find makrut lime leaves, I highly recommend adding them for a bright, fragrant note. It's all tossed in a coconut cream and fish sauce dressing, and goes well alongside Easygoing Flank Steak (page 193), Salmon Burgers with Sesame Chili Mayo (page 159), Gochujang Chicken Wings (page 189), or Roasted Cauliflower with Spicy Miso Tahini & Garlicky Panko (page 177).

2 tbsp coconut cream (like Savoy) or from the top of an unshaken can of coconut milk (like Aroy-D)

1 tbsp maple syrup

2 tsp GF fish sauce

2 tsp lime juice

4 cobs corn, husks removed

1 tbsp neutral high-heat cooking oil

2 makrut lime leaves, stems removed, finely chopped, or 1 tsp lime zest

2 sprigs fresh mint, chopped

2 sprigs fresh basil (Thai or Italian), chopped

1 red bell pepper, finely diced

1 jalapeño, minced (remove seeds and pith for less spice)

¼ red onion, thinly sliced

PLANT-BASED OPTION
Fish sauce → GF soy sauce or tamari

1. In a large bowl, whisk together the coconut cream, maple syrup, fish sauce, and lime juice.

2. Preheat a cleaned grill to high heat (500°F/260°C) or the broiler to high.

3. Brush the corn with oil and char directly on the grill or on a baking sheet in the oven for 10 minutes, rotating occasionally, until the corn has speckles of black, flavorful char. Let cool until cool enough to touch.

4. On a cutting board, place the corn cobs on their side (not standing up!), and cut the corn kernels off the cob, rotating as necessary.

5. Stir in the lime leaves, mint, basil, bell peppers, jalapeños, and red onions. Serve immediately.

ROASTED VEG QUINOA BOWLS

with Lemon Ginger Vinaigrette

SERVES 4

Inspired by the search for balance

♫ *Crave You (feat. Giselle) – Flight Facilities*

I try to live my life in balance, inside and outside of the kitchen. As much as I love to eat decadently, I also have a deep appreciation for nourishing, feel-good meals that don't compromise on flavor. Gluten-free eating is too often tied to sacrificing the enjoyment of food, but that's not my approach. These quinoa bowls are vibrant, tasty, and revitalizing. The Lemon Ginger Vinaigrette complements a wide range of vegetables and proteins, making it a versatile option for any salad or grain bowl. Feel free to switch up the Lemon Ginger Vinaigrette with any other dressing from pages 26–28.

1 large sweet potato, peeled, quartered, and cut into ½-inch-thick slices

2 tbsp neutral high-heat cooking oil

½ tsp mild paprika

½ tsp garlic powder

½ tsp kosher salt

1 cup quinoa (½ cup red and ½ cup white, for color variation), rinsed

2 cups unsalted vegetable stock

1 yellow bell pepper, cut into 1-inch squares

1 red bell pepper, cut into 1-inch squares

1 large zucchini, halved lengthwise and sliced into thick half moons

½ red onion, cut into 1-inch squares

4 small handfuls of mixed leafy greens

Lemon Ginger Vinaigrette (page 27) to taste

Fresh cilantro, chopped (optional)

½ lemon, cut into wedges (optional)

1. Preheat the oven to 400°F (200°C). Line two baking sheets with parchment paper.

2. In a large bowl, toss the sweet potatoes in half each of the oil, paprika, garlic powder, and salt. Spread out in a single layer on one of the prepared pans. Roast, setting a timer for 10 minutes.

3. Meanwhile, in a medium saucepan, combine the quinoa and stock and bring to a simmer on low heat. Cover and simmer for 18 minutes or until all of the stock is absorbed. Turn off the heat and keep covered on the stove until ready to serve.

4. In the same bowl used to toss the sweet potatoes, toss the bell peppers, zucchini, and onions in the remaining oil, paprika, garlic powder, and salt. Spread out in a single layer on the second prepared pan.

5. When the timer goes off, turn the sweet potatoes, place the second pan of vegetables on a separate rack, and roast for 10 minutes or until the sweet potatoes and other vegetables are just tender and golden.

6. Portion the quinoa into bowls. Top with the leafy greens, roasted sweet potatoes, and roasted vegetables. Dress each bowl with 1 to 2 tablespoons of the vinaigrette. Garnish with cilantro and lemon wedges, if using.

NOTE

For added protein, try topping this salad with Sesame Tuna Steaks with Ponzu (page 190), Cha Siu Chicken (page 186), Caramelized Sweet Chili Shrimp (page 185), or Easygoing Flank Steak (page 193) before dressing with the vinaigrette.

TENDER KALE, ASIAN PEAR & BUTTERNUT SQUASH

with Feta & Fried Shallot Dressing

SERVES 4

Inspired by squash season
and sweater weather
♫ *Candied Tangerines
– Jon Bryant and Two Another*

An autumn salad, but with an Asian-Canadian twist, of course. Here, tender massaged kale, roasted butternut squash, creamy feta, crisp Asian pears, and crunchy walnuts come together for a mixture of delightful textures. The dressing, made by blending fried GF shallots, imparts a delicious roasty flavor to every ingredient it clings to.

1 small butternut squash, peeled, seeded, and cut into ½-inch cubes

1 tbsp neutral high-heat cooking oil

½ tsp kosher salt

½ tsp garlic powder

½ tsp mild paprika

4 leaves lacinato or curly kale, thick stems removed, shredded

Fried Shallot Dressing (page 27)

1 Asian pear or crisp apple (such as Honeycrisp), peeled and julienned

½ cup toasted walnut halves (see page 25)

¼ cup crumbled feta cheese

1 tbsp GF fried shallots

DAIRY-FREE/PLANT-BASED OPTION

Feta → 12 pitted green olives (Castelvetrano), roughly chopped

1. Preheat the oven to 400°F (200°C). Line a baking sheet with parchment paper.

2. In a large bowl, combine the squash, oil, salt, garlic powder, and paprika. Spread out in a single layer on the prepared pan. Roast for 30 minutes, tossing halfway through, until golden brown around the edges. Set aside to cool to room temperature.

3. Meanwhile, in a large bowl, combine the kale and about 2 tablespoons of the shallot dressing. Using your hands, gently massage until fully coated and tender.

4. Add the cooled squash and the Asian pears to the kale. Dress to taste and gently toss with tongs or salad servers. Garnish with the walnuts, feta, and fried shallots.

NOTE

When making a kale salad, always dress and massage the kale before combining it with the other ingredients. This ensures your kale is tender, especially when it's winter and the leaves are especially tough and hearty.

CHARRED ROMAINE
with Silken Tofu Caesar Dressing

Inspired by good ol' classic
Caesar salad

♫ *Lovely Day/Good as Hell
Mashup - Pomplamoose*

SERVES 6

Caesar salad, done JLo style (but not *that* JLo)! This version features smoky, charred romaine halves, with the addition of burst cherry tomatoes and crisp cucumber slices because I like a Caesar with more than just lettuce. Keep the ends intact; this is a knife-and-fork kind of salad! The star of the show is the plant-based tofu dressing, packed with flavor from the fermented black beans, chili paste, and toasted sesame oil. Instead of traditional gluten-filled croutons, it's topped with fried shallots for crunch. Serve as a light lunch or with a grilled protein like Cha Siu Chicken (page 186) or Sesame Tuna Steaks with Ponzu (page 190).

A drizzle of neutral high-heat cooking oil

3 romaine hearts, each halved lengthwise with the ends intact

Silken Tofu Caesar Dressing (page 28)

1 pint cherry tomatoes, halved

½ English cucumber, sliced into half moons

6 tbsp GF fried shallots

Grated Parmesan cheese

Fresh cilantro, chopped (optional)

DAIRY-FREE/PLANT-BASED OPTION
Parmesan → nutritional yeast

1. Preheat a cleaned grill to high heat (500°F/260°C).

2. Brush oil onto the flat edge of the romaine hearts and grill flat side down for 15 seconds on a diagonal from the grid. Rotate the romaine to the opposite diagonal to char for 15 seconds for the coveted grill marks (or quadrillage, if you're brushing up on your French kitchen lingo).

3. Smear a large spoonful of dressing across each serving plate. Place a romaine half on each plate. Top with the tomatoes, cucumbers, fried shallots, and Parmesan. Drizzle more dressing over top and garnish with cilantro (if using).

NOTE
This recipe works great when you already have the grill on for something like the Easygoing Flank Steak (page 193), since charring the lettuce only takes about 30 seconds.

MAGIC SPUDS SALAD

SERVES 4 🍴 🌱 🍃

Inspired by Papa Lo

♫ *Stayin' Alive – Lizzy McAlpine and Scary Pockets*

Potato salad holds a special place in my heart, as it was one of the few things my dad cooked during my childhood, and only for the occasional potluck. My sisters and I have a soft spot for his version, which had chopped boiled eggs and a distinct flavor from Miracle Whip. While I'll never be able to replicate his recipe—since it was purely intuitive, with no measurements written down—I present to you my own version, a tribute to the one dish he proudly claimed as his own after immigrating from Hong Kong to Toronto.

DRESSING

½-inch knob ginger, minced

2 tbsp Miracle Whip, or 2 tbsp mayonnaise + ¼ tsp mild paprika + ¼ tsp garlic powder

1 tbsp mirin, or ½ tbsp unsalted cooking sake + ½ tbsp maple syrup

1 tbsp rice vinegar

1 tbsp Dijon or grainy mustard

¼ tsp kosher salt

SALAD

1½ lb (675 g) baby potatoes, halved

2 stalks celery, peeled (see note) and sliced on a diagonal

A few chives, finely chopped

PLANT-BASED OPTION

Miracle Whip → plant-based mayonnaise + ¼ tsp mild paprika + ¼ tsp garlic powder

1. **MAKE THE DRESSING:** In a small bowl, whisk together the ginger, Miracle Whip, mirin, rice vinegar, mustard, and salt. Set aside.

2. **FOR THE SALAD:** Fill a medium to large pot with salted water, using about 2 tablespoons of kosher salt per 4 cups of water, and bring to a boil. Add the potatoes and boil for 10 to 15 minutes, depending on how tender you like them (10 minutes for potatoes with a bit of bite; 15 minutes for a starchier, creamier salad). Drain in a colander and let cool.

3. Add the potatoes to a large bowl and mix with the dressing and celery. Garnish with chives.

4. Let come to room temperature for 30 minutes before serving. Store in an airtight container in the fridge for up to 3 days.

NOTE
For optimal crunch, peel the outer side of each celery stalk with a peeler to remove fibers.

SMACKED CUCUMBER SALAD

SERVES 4 🗡 ☘ 🌿

Inspired by the dumpling houses we frequented in Toronto

♫ *Sweet Emotion – The Kooks*

Here's my gluten-free rendition of Chinese cucumber salad. It's addictively crunchy, comes together in a snap, and can be devoured as a snack or served as a refreshing side to other bold, soy-based dishes like Canto-Style Mapo Tofu (page 106) or Chili Miso Salmon (page 182). Don't skip out on the smacking part: not only is it fun, but it also increases the cucumber's ability to absorb flavor.

4 to 6 Persian or Lebanese cucumbers, ends removed

1 clove garlic, minced, plus more to taste (optional)

½ tsp kosher salt, plus more to taste

2 tsp GF Chinese black vinegar (or see page 13 for sub), plus more to taste

1 tsp GF soy sauce or tamari, plus more to taste

1 tsp toasted sesame oil, plus more to taste

1 tsp GF chili oil (such as chili crisp), plus more to taste

½ tsp maple syrup, plus more to taste

1 tbsp roasted sesame seeds

Fresh cilantro, chopped (optional)

1. Lay out the cucumbers on a cutting board. Using a rolling pin or the dull edge of a chef's knife, smack each cucumber until it splits. Cut lengthwise into quarters, then cut each length on a diagonal into bite-sized pieces.

2. In a large bowl, season the cucumbers with garlic (if using), salt, vinegar, soy sauce, sesame oil, chili oil, and maple syrup. Mix to combine. Adjust the seasonings to taste.

3. Using a slotted spoon, transfer the cucumbers to a serving bowl, leaving behind any liquid to discard. Garnish with the sesame seeds and cilantro (if using). Serve immediately.

SUMMER ROLLS

with Ssamjang

Inspired by Vietnamese fresh rolls
and Korean BBQ

♫ *Kingdom – Maribou State
and North Downs*

MAKES 6 ROLLS 🍸 ☘ 🍃

I love summer rolls as a refreshing snack, but it took some trial and error to master rolling these babies. Luckily for you, I've gathered key tips for crafting beautiful summer rolls in the sidebar on the next page. Traditionally, summer rolls are served with Nuoc Cham (page 29) or a peanut hoisin sauce, which often contains gluten. I like to serve them with gluten-free Ssamjang (page 30), my favorite dipping sauce from Korean BBQ restaurants. Note that ssamjang is quite punchy, so a little goes a long way.

4 oz (115 g) rice vermicelli

6 leaves of leafy lettuce (green, red, oak, Boston, Bibb)

½ red, orange, or yellow bell pepper

¼ English cucumber

12 slices GF kimchi

6 sprigs fresh cilantro, basil (Thai or Italian), and/or mint leaves

Fresh edible flowers (optional)

6 large or jumbo shrimp, peeled, deveined, and halved lengthwise (see note on page 83)

A drizzle of toasted sesame oil

Six 9-inch round rice paper wrappers

Ssamjang (page 30)

½ lime, cut into wedges (optional)

PLANT-BASED OPTION

- Shrimp → 4 oz (115 g) GF fried or firm tofu, thinly sliced
- Check the kimchi ingredients for seafood products

1. In a large bowl, soak the vermicelli in cool water for 30 minutes.

2. **MEANWHILE, PREPARE THE FILLING INGREDIENTS:** Remove the crunchy ends of the lettuce. Julienne the bell pepper and cucumber. Chop the kimchi. Assemble on a large platter with the herbs and edible flowers.

3. Bring a large pot of salted water to boil. Blanch the shrimp until pink, firm, and opaque, about 2 minutes. Using a slotted spoon, transfer to a bowl with ice to cool.

4. Drain the vermicelli. In the same pot, blanch the vermicelli for 1 to 2 minutes, then taste test for doneness: it should be tender but still have resistance. Drain in a colander and run under cold water. Toss in a drizzle of sesame oil to prevent clumping. Drain the shrimp and let dry.

5. **SET UP YOUR WRAPPING STATION:** Fill a deep pan or dish wide enough to fit a full summer roll wrapper with cool water. Set up a cutting board as your rolling station, with the platter of fillings alongside.

6. Submerge a rice paper wrapper in the water for 2 seconds and lay it out on your cutting board. It will still feel stiff, but will soften as you fill it with ingredients. Use your palm to swipe across the rice paper onto the board, pressing it so that it doesn't curl off the board.

7. Place a piece of lettuce in the center of the bottom half of the wrapper. On top of the lettuce, place one-sixth each of the vermicelli, cucumbers, bell peppers, and kimchi. Roll into a lettuce wrap sitting on top of the flat rice paper wrapper.

8. In the rice paper roll, outside and above the lettuce wrap, lay out a row of the shrimp, one-sixth of the herbs, and two or three edible flowers, pretty side down. This is what you'll see once the summer rolls are rolled.

CONTINUED

9. Fold the bottom of the rice paper wrapper over the lettuce wrap, then fold in each side. Roll up snugly from the bottom over the shrimp, herbs, and flowers.

10. Repeat with the remaining wrappers, lettuce, and fillings. Cut each roll in half. Serve with the ssamjang and lime wedges (if using).

FOR TIGHT SUMMER ROLLS:

- Soak the rice papers in cool water instead of hot, and only soak them for a couple seconds. Hot water can make the papers more challenging to roll and prone to tearing.

- To keep the rolls tight and neat, wrap the majority of the filling in a delicate lettuce leaf.

- Place visually appealing ingredients, such as herbs or edible flowers, outside the lettuce wrap so they directly touch the rice paper. This ensures they'll be visible once the roll is complete.

- Place the prepared rolls on a parchment-lined platter or baking sheet. Cover with a damp (not dripping-wet) kitchen towel to prevent them from drying out.

- To prevent the rolls from sticking together, cut an English cucumber into four equal lengths and shave each length (preferably with a mandoline) into thin sheets to use as dividers between the rolls.

NOURISHING SOUPS

When I was growing up, every dinner ended with a steaming bowl of nourishing broth. Between Mama, Gong (my grandpa), and Poh (my grandma), someone always had a pot of soup simmering away throughout the day, filling our home with a medley of distinct, medicinal aromas.

Mama still has a deep drawer of jars and containers filled with dried fruits, plants, seeds, and barks, and whenever I go home, there is always a bowl of tong (bone broth) waiting for me—an instant mouthful of cozy sustenance. A bowl of love. The elixir, a combination of Chinese herbs and pork bones, remedies any condition needing attention, from rebalancing qi to boosting the immune system. I'm still learning what's in that magical drawer of hers and will do my best to preserve this tradition in my own kitchen. Even though I'm still discovering the power of these Chinese herbs and broths, I very much inherited the Asian mom characteristic of wanting to cure every ailment in the world with hot liquid.

Soups are the ultimate expression of care for yourself and others. They're often overlooked or labeled boring, but what's better than a miraculous concoction of rich colors and flavors to brighten the day and soothe the soul? By harnessing the power of a well-stocked gluten-free pantry, complemented by a few select items from the store, you can delve into an expansive world of soups, from the comforting warmth of Turmeric & Rice Chicken Soup (page 79) to the classic Hot & Sour Soup (page 88).

Soups are remarkably versatile and adaptable to whatever ingredients you have on hand. If you're just getting into cooking, start with soup! It's the easiest way to get comfortable in the kitchen and connect with your senses while nourishing your body and mind.

Scan me to
listen along!

TOM YUM CORN CHOWDER

SERVES 4 TO 6 🥄 🌱 🍃

Inspired by wok-fried baby corn after a trek in Thailand
♫ *Animal Spirits – Vulfpeck*

This is one of those dishes that perfectly embodies the way I love to cook: playing with classic North American dishes (chowder), highlighting the freshest produce available (corn), and incorporating bright and bold Asian flavors (tom yum). This punchy soup draws inspiration from the best corn I've ever eaten, combining the essence of delectable in-season corn with zesty Thai flavors.

2 large cobs corn, husks removed

2 tbsp neutral high-heat cooking oil

2 sweet potatoes (about 1 lb/450 g), finely diced

2 cloves garlic, minced

2 stalks lemongrass, white parts only, smashed (see note)

1 jalapeño, minced (keep the seeds for an extra kick)

2-inch knob ginger, minced

4 cups unsalted chicken stock, vegetable stock, or Freezer Bag Stock (page 24)

1 tsp kosher salt

1 red bell pepper, finely diced

1 can (14 oz/400 ml) full-fat coconut milk

½ tbsp maple syrup

2 tbsp tom yum paste or Thai red curry paste

2 tsp chili paste (such as sambal oelek or Calabrian)

2 tbsp lime juice (about 1 lime)

Fresh cilantro or basil (Thai or Italian), chopped (optional)

PLANT-BASED NOTE
Check for seafood products in the tom yum or curry paste

1. Cut the corn kernels off the cobs (you should have about 2 cups) and set both the cobs and the kernels aside.

2. In a medium stock pot or Dutch oven, heat the oil on medium heat until it shimmers. Add the sweet potatoes, garlic, lemongrass, jalapeños, and ginger and sauté for 2 to 3 minutes, until the sweet potatoes are beginning to soften and the aromatics become fragrant.

3. Stir in the stock and salt. Add the corn cobs (not the kernels), lower the heat to medium-low, and simmer for 15 minutes or until the sweet potatoes are fork-tender, stirring occasionally. Using tongs, remove and discard the lemongrass and corn cobs.

4. Add half each of the corn kernels and red peppers to the pot, along with the coconut milk, maple syrup, tom yum paste, and chili paste and simmer for 5 minutes, stirring occasionally. Turn off the heat and stir in the lime juice.

5. Using an immersion blender in the pot, blend the soup, keeping it chunky. (Or ladle half of the soup into a stand blender and blitz, keeping it chunky. Return the soup to the pot.)

6. Add the remaining corn and red peppers and heat on medium heat for 5 minutes or until slightly reduced, stirring a few times.

7. Ladle into soup bowls and, if using, garnish with cilantro.

NOTES
In-season corn is optimal, but frozen corn is your best bet for the rest of the year. Since it's flash-frozen at peak harvest, frozen corn keeps its natural sweetness and adds more flavor to the soup than out-of-season corn on the cob. Canned corn is too soft and will not provide the same burst of freshness.

Use the dull edge of a chef's knife or a rolling pin to smash the lemongrass. If you can't find lemongrass, stir in 2 tsp lemon zest with the lime juice.

RICE CAKE SOUP

with Ground Pork & Spinach

SERVES 2 🌶️ 🌱 🍃

Inspired by Asian Legend, a Shanghainese restaurant chain in Toronto

♫ Losing My Way – FKJ and Tom Misch

Shanghainese rice cake soups take me back to the many family outings we had in North Toronto during my childhood. Our neighborhood was a complete haven of regional Chinese cuisines, and it was only after leaving for culinary school in Montreal that I truly appreciated how good I had it. I love rice cakes for their ability to soak up flavors with their tender, chewy texture. I always pick up a bag of gluten-free rice cakes when I find them at the store, since they're not always available and some standard rice cakes still contain wheat. This soup is a great cozy weekday meal, building quick flavor from simple and readily available ingredients.

2 tbsp neutral high-heat cooking oil, plus more as needed

4 oz (115 g) cremini mushrooms, stems removed and caps sliced

8 oz (225 g) lean or medium ground pork

¼ tsp kosher salt, plus more to taste

2 scallions, white and green parts separated, chopped

½-inch knob ginger, sliced into thin matchsticks

2 tbsp unsalted cooking wine or sake

2 cups unsalted chicken stock, vegetable stock, or Freezer Bag Stock (page 24)

1 cup GF Chinese or Korean rice cakes (see note)

1 cup spinach, roughly chopped

½ tbsp rice vinegar

Freshly cracked black pepper to taste

2 tbsp GF fried garlic (optional)

A drizzle of GF chili oil (such as chili crisp) (optional)

Fresh cilantro, chopped (optional)

PLANT-BASED/PESCATARIAN OPTION

Ground pork → plant-based ground round (such as Beyond or Impossible)

1. In a medium saucepan or wok, heat 1 tablespoon of the cooking oil on medium-high heat until it shimmers. Add the mushrooms and sauté for 2 to 3 minutes, until browned. If the pan gets dry, drizzle in a bit more oil. Transfer the mushrooms to a bowl and set aside.

2. Reduce the heat to medium. Add the remaining oil to the pan, then add the pork and salt. Sauté for 3 to 4 minutes, breaking up the pork with a wooden spoon, until browned and just cooked through. Add the white scallions and ginger and sauté for 1 minute or until fragrant. Add the cooking wine and cook, scraping up any browned bits, until the liquid has evaporated.

3. Return the mushrooms to the pan and stir in the stock and rice cakes. Reduce the heat to medium-low, cover, and simmer for 10 minutes, stirring occasionally, until the rice cakes are tender with a slight chew.

4. Stir in the spinach and green scallions and simmer, uncovered, for 2 minutes or until wilted but still bright green. Stir in the vinegar. Season with salt and black pepper.

5. Ladle into soup bowls and, if using, garnish with fried garlic, chili oil, and cilantro.

NOTE

Rice cakes can be found in the fridge, next to the tofu, at your local Asian grocery store. Most rice cakes are gluten-free, as they're traditionally made with rice flour, water, oil, and salt, but double-check the ingredient list, as some contain wheat starch. If you can't find GF rice cakes, you can substitute with GF gnocchi. The rice cakes or gnocchi will release some starch and thicken the soup naturally. If it is too thick for your liking at the end of step 4, add a bit more stock and season to taste.

COCONUT CURRY NOODLE SOUP

Inspired by khao soi

♫ *All We Need*
(feat. Shy Girls) – ODESZA

SERVES 4 🐟 🌱 🍃

This luscious and spicy noodle soup is a big, warm embrace when you need it, with bone-in chicken simmered in a coconut curry broth until it's pull-apart tender. Reid and I first devoured a similar gluten-free version of khao soi after hunting it down in Chiang Mai. Traditionally, it's served with gluten-filled egg noodles with a generous topping of deep-fried egg noodles for added crunch. This recipe opts for thin rice noodles and a mound of gluten-free crispy shallots instead.

10½ oz (300 g) dried thin (⅛-inch) flat rice noodles

2 cans (14 oz/400 ml each) full-fat coconut milk, one can unshaken (see note)

1 tbsp neutral high-heat cooking oil, plus more for drizzling

4 cloves garlic, minced

2 small shallots, minced (about ¼ cup)

¼ cup Thai red curry paste

4 cups unsalted chicken stock, vegetable stock, or Freezer Bag Stock (page 24)

4 bone-in, skin-on chicken legs (about 2 lb/900 g total), divided into thigh and drum pieces

4 makrut lime leaves, crumbled (see note)

1 tbsp brown sugar

1 tsp kosher salt

2 tbsp GF fish sauce, soy sauce, or tamari

12 to 16 stalks baby gai lan or Shanghai bok choy, ends trimmed

1 cup GF fried shallots

Fresh mint, basil (Thai or Italian), and/or cilantro, chopped

½ lime, cut into wedges

A drizzle of GF chili oil (such as chili crisp)

1. In a large bowl, soak the rice noodles in cool water for at least 30 minutes. (This allows them to blanch quickly without turning gloppy.)

2. Meanwhile, open the unshaken can of coconut milk and remove ¼ cup of cream from the top. In a large pot, heat the coconut cream and cooking oil on medium heat until lightly bubbling. Add the garlic, shallots, and curry paste and sauté until very fragrant, about 1 to 2 minutes.

3. Stir in the remaining coconut cream, coconut milk, stock, chicken, lime leaves, brown sugar, salt, and fish sauce. Bring to a boil, then reduce the heat to low, cover, and simmer gently for 30 minutes, stirring occasionally. Turn off the heat.

4. Wait for 20 minutes, then bring another large pot of salted water to a boil. Add a drizzle of oil (this will make the gai lan glossy). Add the gai lan and cook until crisp-tender, about 1 to 2 minutes. Using tongs, transfer the gai lan to a large bowl.

5. Bring the water back to a boil and blanch the rice noodles until soft yet chewy, about 1 to 3 minutes, checking frequently for doneness. Drain in a colander and run under cold water. Toss the noodles in a drizzle of oil to prevent them from clumping, then portion into four soup bowls.

6. Using tongs, remove the chicken pieces from the broth—you can shred them into bite-sized pieces for easier eating. Divide the chicken among the bowls and ladle in the hot broth. Garnish with fried shallots and chopped herbs. Serve with lime wedges and chili oil on the side.

PLANT-BASED/PESCATARIAN OPTION

- Chicken legs → 8 oz (225 g) GF fried tofu, cubed, or tofu puffs + 1 lb (450 g) mushrooms (such as cremini, shiitake, or oyster), stems removed and caps sliced

- Check for seafood products in the curry paste (disregard if pescatarian)

NOTES

Be sure not to shake the can of coconut milk, so that the top cream layer remains separate from the milk.

If you can't find makrut lime leaves, stir in 2 tsp lime zest at the end of step 3.

SWEET POTATO & CAULIFLOWER PURÉE

with Chinese Sausage

SERVES 4 TO 6 🐟 🌱 🌿

Inspired by Gong's
use of Chinese sausage

♫ *Better Man – Leon Bridges*

In traditional Chinese cuisine, puréed soups exist only as desserts (think sweet black sesame or almond soup). But the jook sing (slang for "North American") in me loves a smooth puréed soup with buttered toast. This soup has a nice kick from Korean chili flakes (gochugaru) and develops deep flavors from anchovies. Once blended, it's served as a base for caramelized Chinese sausage (a favorite ingredient Gong often brought home in links), roasty fried garlic, and a drizzle of fruity olive oil.

1 tbsp neutral high-heat cooking oil, plus more for the sausage

4 anchovy fillets

2 cloves garlic, sliced

1 large yellow onion, diced

2 sweet potatoes, diced

1 lb (450 g) cauliflower, chopped into small florets

6 cups unsalted chicken stock, vegetable stock, or Freezer Bag Stock (page 24)

2 tbsp GF miso paste

½ tsp unsalted Korean chili flakes (gochugaru) or Kashmiri chili powder

2 links GF Chinese sausage (lap cheong), sliced on a diagonal or cubed (see note)

1½ tsp rice vinegar

Kosher salt to taste

¼ cup GF fried garlic

Fresh cilantro and/or scallions, chopped (optional)

A drizzle of extra virgin olive oil

PLANT-BASED/PESCATARIAN OPTION

- Anchovies → 4 kalamata olives, chopped, or 2 tsp chopped drained capers (disregard if pescatarian)
- Omit the Chinese sausage

SUB

If you can't find gochugaru or Kashmiri chili powder, use ½ tsp mild paprika + ⅛ tsp cayenne

1. In a medium stock pot or Dutch oven, heat the cooking oil on medium heat until it shimmers. Add the anchovies, garlic, and onions and sauté for 2 to 3 minutes to release aromas.

2. Stir in the sweet potatoes, cauliflower, stocsk, miso, and chili flakes. Reduce the heat to low, cover, and simmer for 20 to 25 minutes, stirring occasionally, until the sweet potatoes and cauliflower are very tender. Turn off the heat and leave on the stove.

3. Meanwhile, in a small nonstick frying pan, heat a very light drizzle of cooking oil on medium heat until it shimmers. Add the sausages and sauté until the fat renders and the sausages begin to crisp, about 5 to 6 minutes. Transfer to a plate lined with a paper towel.

4. Using an immersion blender in the pot, purée the soup until uniform in consistency. (Or carefully transfer it to a stand blender, in batches if needed, purée, and then return to the pot.) Stir in the rice vinegar and salt.

5. Ladle into soup bowls and garnish with the sausages, fried garlic, herbs (if using), and olive oil.

NOTE

It can be hard to find GF Chinese sausages (lap cheong), as they typically contain soy sauce, but the sweetness of maple-flavored bacon can easily sub in: use 2 slices, cut into small strips. You can also use 2 links of Spanish chorizo, which has a similar texture but a smokier taste.

TURMERIC & RICE CHICKEN SOUP

SERVES 4 🐓 🌿 🌱

Inspired by a cooking
class in Chiang Mai

♫ *The Spirit Blossoms All
Over the Land – Onra*

This soup was inspired by a chef named We whom Reid and I met in Thailand. Before guiding us through the wet market to gather ingredients for the day, she fed us each a bowl of flavorful rice soup made with pork, chilies, and loads of herbs that sustained us through the afternoon. This version features ground chicken and turmeric, my hybrid of chicken noodle soup and congee. It's a scrappy way to repurpose leftover rice, and it's the perfect pick-me-up when you're feeling under the weather. When I'm extra hungry, I like to serve it with jammy soft-boiled eggs, so I've included them in this recipe, but they can easily be omitted.

2 tbsp neutral high-heat cooking oil

1 lb (450 g) ground chicken

6 sprigs fresh cilantro, separated into leaves and stems, chopped

2 cloves garlic, minced

2 carrots, diced

2 large celery stalks, diced

1 yellow onion, diced

1-inch knob ginger, minced

1 tbsp Thai red or yellow curry paste (see curry paste on page 14)

½ tsp ground turmeric

4 cups unsalted chicken stock, vegetable stock, or Freezer Bag Stock (page 24)

4 large eggs

1 cup cooked rice (see page 24)

2 sprigs fresh basil (Thai or Italian) and/or scallions, chopped

GF fried garlic, to garnish

Kosher salt and freshly cracked black pepper to taste

PLANT-BASED/PESCATARIAN OPTION

- Chicken → plant-based ground round (such as Beyond or Impossible)
- Omit the eggs

1. In a medium stock pot or Dutch oven, heat the oil on medium heat until it shimmers. Add the chicken and sauté for 3 to 4 minutes, breaking it up with a wooden spoon, until browned. Add the cilantro stems, garlic, carrots, celery, onions, ginger, curry paste, and turmeric and sauté for 5 minutes.

2. Stir in the stock and bring to a boil. Reduce the heat to low, cover, leaving the lid ajar, and simmer for 15 minutes, stirring occasionally.

3. Meanwhile, in a small pot of boiling water, boil the eggs for 7 minutes. Fill a large bowl with cold water. Using a slotted spoon, transfer the soft-boiled eggs into the cold water to shock them. Peel the eggs and slice in half lengthwise.

4. Stir the cooked rice into the soup and simmer, uncovered, for a few minutes to let the rice heat through and take on flavor.

5. Ladle the soup into bowls and top with the eggs, cilantro leaves, basil, and fried garlic. Season with salt and pepper.

NOTE

Instead of browning ground chicken, you can add leftover cooked chicken with the stock.

QUICK MISO (NOODLE) SOUP

Inspired by gluten-free yuzu shio ramen at AFURI

♫ *California – The Lagoons*

SERVES 2

It can be unclear at restaurants whether their miso soup contains gluten. With this super-quick broth, you can start your takeaway sushi meal with a restaurant-quality bowl of soup, just like everyone else. To transform it into a complete meal, simply add noodles and your favorite effortless protein. Kimchi and preserved citrus add layers of bold flavor, but they're not essential to the dish.

4 cups water

2 tbsp dried wakame (seaweed)

1 tbsp hondashi (see note)

1 tbsp unsalted cooking wine or sake

4 oz (115 g) mushrooms (such as cremini, oyster, shiitake, and/or shimeji), stems removed and caps sliced

1 scallion, white and green parts separated, chopped

½ yellow onion, sliced

5 oz (140 g) 100% buckwheat soba noodles or dried GF spaghetti

A drizzle of extra virgin olive oil

8 oz (225 g) cooked chicken, shredded, or soft tofu, cubed

4 leaves napa cabbage or other Asian greens, chopped

1 tbsp GF miso paste

2 tbsp GF chopped kimchi (optional)

1 tsp yuzu paste or chopped preserved lemon, or a squeeze of lemon juice (optional)

PLANT-BASED OPTION

Omit the hondashi, which contains dried fish

1. In a medium pot, combine the water, wakame, hondashi, cooking wine, mushrooms, white scallions, and onions. Bring to a boil, then reduce the heat to low, cover, and simmer for 15 minutes, stirring occasionally, allowing the flavorings to infuse into a broth.

2. Meanwhile, cook the noodles according to package instructions. If using soba noodles, stir frequently, as they're prone to sticking together. Drain in a colander and rinse under cool water. Drizzle with a bit of olive oil to prevent clumping.

3. Add the chicken and cabbage to the broth and simmer, uncovered, for 2 minutes. Turn off the heat and dissolve the miso in the broth (this is added at the end to preserve the miso's flavor and nutrients). If using, stir in the kimchi and yuzu paste.

4. Divide the noodles and miso broth into noodle soup bowls. Add the protein and greens and garnish with green scallions.

NOTES

Some hondashis contain yeast extract, which may be spooky for celiacs to see, but in Canada and the US, the manufacturer is required to list any common allergens present, and gluten itself is usually not listed. If you're not comfortable using hondashi, omit it and increase the miso paste to 2 tablespoons.

For a side or appetizer soup, skip on the cabbage and noodles, and use a total of 4 oz (115 g) cubed soft tofu.

MACARONI LAKSA

SERVES 4 🐟 🌱 🌿

Inspired by
Malaysian hawker centers and
Hong Kong macaroni soup
🎵 I Wanna Go – Yuna

I first fell in love with laksa in Penang, Malaysia, at my first hawker center, where the scents were tantalizing and the live karaoke went all night long. While most laksa stalls offer a choice between egg and rice noodles, people with gluten allergies would find it challenging to avoid cross-contamination. This recipe brings together the flavors of my all-time favorite broth with the spoonability of Hong Kong–style macaroni soup. It strikes my ideal balance of funk, spice, richness, and tang. For a traditional version, simply make it with rice noodles instead of macaroni.

2 cans (14 oz/400 ml each) full-fat coconut milk, one can unshaken (see note on page 13)

1 tbsp neutral high-heat cooking oil

4 cloves garlic, minced

1 small shallot, minced (about 2 tbsp)

1-inch knob ginger, grated or minced

3 tbsp shrimp paste, or 6 anchovies

3 tbsp Thai red curry paste

4 cups unsalted chicken stock, vegetable stock, or Freezer Bag Stock (page 24)

1 tbsp maple syrup

1 tsp kosher salt

2 makrut lime leaves, crumbled (see note)

8 oz (225 g) GF fried tofu, cubed, or tofu puffs

8 oz (225 g) large or jumbo shrimp, peeled and deveined (see note)

2 tbsp lime juice (about 1 lime)

FIXINGS

8 oz (225 g) GF fish balls

12 to 16 stalks gai lan or other Asian greens

2 cups dried GF macaroni

A drizzle of extra virgin olive oil

Fresh cilantro and/or scallions, chopped (optional)

GF fried shallots or garlic (optional)

½ long red Thai chili, thinly sliced (optional)

PLANT-BASED OPTION

· Shrimp paste → 1 tbsp GF miso paste

· Shrimp → hearty mushrooms, stems removed and kept whole

· Fish balls → additional fried tofu

1. Open the unshaken can of coconut milk and remove ¼ cup of cream from the top. In a large pot, heat the coconut cream and cooking oil on medium-high heat until lightly bubbling. Add the garlic, shallots, ginger, shrimp paste, and curry paste and sauté for 2 minutes or until fragrant.

2. Stir in the remaining coconut cream, coconut milk, stock, maple syrup, salt, and lime leaves. Bring to a boil, then reduce the heat to a simmer. Add the tofu and simmer for 10 minutes, stirring occasionally. Add the shrimp and simmer for 1 to 2 minutes, or until pink, firm, and opaque. Turn off the heat and stir in the lime juice.

3. **MEANWHILE, PREPARE YOUR FIXINGS:** Bring a large pot of salted water to a boil. Add the fish balls and gai lan and blanch for 2 to 3 minutes, until the fish balls are floating and the gai lan is crisp-tender. Using a slotted spoon or tongs, transfer the fish balls and gai lan to a bowl.

4. Add the macaroni to the pot of boiling water and cook for 1 minute less than the package instructions (it will continue to cook in the hot broth). Drain in a colander and drizzle with olive oil to prevent sticking.

5. Transfer the macaroni into noodle soup bowls. Ladle the broth, tofu, and shrimp into the bowls. Add the fish balls and gai lan. If using, garnish with cilantro, fried shallots, and chilies.

NOTES

If you can't find makrut lime leaves, stir in 1 tsp lime zest with the lime juice.

If using frozen shrimp, thaw them first in a bowl of cold water for 10 to 20 minutes, then drain.

Any leftover broth can be frozen for up to 3 months and defrosted for a quick meal.

MISO CREAM-OF MUSHROOM SOUP

Inspired by Dad's love
of mushroom soup

♫ *My Girl – The Temptations*

SERVES 4 🐟 🌱 🍃

Here's a creamy mushroom soup without cream, since my parents didn't acclimatize to consuming much dairy beyond Hong Kong milk tea. If you haven't already noticed, I love using miso paste to create quick flavor, and that's definitely the case here. Unlike traditional French soups that rely on a roux (a mixture of flour and butter) for thickening, this soup achieves its velvety texture by blending copious amounts of earthy mushrooms in an umami-rich stock.

4 tbsp neutral high-heat cooking oil

1½ lb (675 g) mixed fresh mushrooms (such as cremini, shiitake, and oyster), stems removed and caps sliced

1 yellow onion, diced

1 scallion, white and green parts separated, chopped

2 cloves garlic, sliced

¼ cup dry white wine

4 cups unsalted chicken stock, vegetable stock, or Freezer Bag Stock (page 24)

4 tsp GF miso paste

¼ tsp freshly cracked black or white pepper, plus more to sprinkle

1 tbsp butter

1 tsp rice vinegar

Kosher salt to taste

DAIRY-FREE/PLANT-BASED OPTION

Butter → plant-based butter (or omit)

1. In a medium stock pot or Dutch oven, heat the oil on medium-high heat until it shimmers. Add the mushrooms and sauté, tossing frequently, until browned, about 3 to 4 minutes. Reduce the heat to medium, add the onions and white scallions, and sauté for 1 minute. Add the garlic and sauté for 1 minute. Add the wine and cook, scraping up any browned bits (called fond) with a wooden spoon, until the liquid has evaporated.

2. Stir in the stock, miso, and pepper. Reduce the heat to low, cover, leaving the lid ajar, and simmer for 30 minutes, stirring occasionally. Turn off the heat and leave on the stove.

3. Using an immersion blender in the pot, purée the soup, leaving tiny mushroom bits: don't blend it completely. (Or carefully transfer it to a stand blender, in batches if needed, purée, leaving tiny mushroom bits, and then return to the pot.) Stir in the butter, rice vinegar, and salt.

4. Ladle into soup bowls and sprinkle with pepper. Garnish with the green scallions.

NOTE
Save the mushroom stems for Freezer Bag Stock (page 24).

TURMERIC & DILL SOUP WITH SAUSAGE, POTATO & KALE

SERVES 4 🍴 🌱 🌿

Inspired by Italian wedding soup and chả cá lã vọng

♫ *Mixer – Amber Mark*

This dish combines the heartiness of Italian wedding soup and the flavors of chả cá lã vọng, a Northern Vietnamese fish dish seasoned with healthy amounts of turmeric and dill. I typically reach for this soup on chilly days for a boost of warmth and sustenance. Best served with buttery toast—we love the gluten-free bread from Promise, Little Northern Bakehouse, Canyon Bakehouse, or Schär.

1 tbsp neutral high-heat cooking oil

1 lb (450 g) GF honey garlic sausages (about 4), casings removed (see note)

1 lb (450 g) baby potatoes, thinly sliced into medallions

4 cloves garlic, minced

2 small shallots, minced (about ¼ cup)

1-inch knob ginger, minced

½ tsp ground turmeric

1 can (14 oz/400 ml) full-fat coconut milk

4 cups unsalted chicken stock, vegetable stock, or Freezer Bag Stock (page 24)

3 leaves lacinato or curly kale, thick stems removed, shredded

2 tsp GF fish sauce, soy sauce, or tamari

Juice of ½ to 1 lime, to taste

6 sprigs fresh dill, chopped

PLANT-BASED/PESCATARIAN OPTION

Sausages → plant-based sausages (such as Beyond or Impossible), cut into medallions

1. In a medium stock pot or Dutch oven, heat the oil on medium-high heat until it shimmers. Add the sausage meat and sauté for 4 minutes, breaking it up with a wooden spoon, until browned. Add the potatoes, garlic, shallots, ginger, and turmeric. Sauté for 2 to 3 minutes to release the flavors.

2. Stir in the coconut milk and stock. Bring to a boil, then reduce the heat to low and simmer for 20 minutes, stirring occasionally. Add the kale and simmer for 5 minutes, stirring a few times, until just tender and still bright green. Turn off the heat and stir in the fish sauce and lime juice.

3. Ladle into soup bowls and garnish with dill.

NOTE

To remove sausages from their casings, snip one end of each sausage with scissors to create an opening, then squeeze out the seasoned meat. Alternatively, use a chef's knife to slice each sausage from one end to the other, then peel away the casing.

HOT & SOUR SOUP

SERVES 4 🍗 🥬 🍴 🌿

Inspired by days spent in Markham, Ontario

♫ *Night Fever – Bee Gees*

This is one of those traditional dishes that's super easy to whip up using gluten-free pantry items, but you won't find many restaurants offering a gluten-free version. For me, hot and sour soup is reminiscent of lunches at dumpling shops with Mama and Papa, a go-to order eaten with gluten-filled versions of Minced Pork Noodles with Cucumbers (page 151) and addictively crunchy Smacked Cucumber Salad (page 63).

2 tbsp neutral high-heat cooking oil

4 oz (115 g) mushrooms (such as cremini, shiitake, oyster, or shimeji), stems removed and caps sliced

2 scallions, white and green parts separated, chopped

½-inch knob ginger, minced

4 cups unsalted chicken stock, vegetable stock, or Freezer Bag Stock (page 24)

4 oz (115 g) firm tofu or GF fried tofu, cubed

2½ oz (70 g) sliced drained bamboo shoots (about ¼ of an 8 oz/225 g can), or 1 carrot, julienned

2 tbsp rice vinegar

2 tbsp GF soy sauce or tamari

1 tsp brown sugar

1 tsp freshly cracked black or white pepper

2 tsp chili paste (such as sambal oelek or Calabrian), or 1 tsp harissa

3 tbsp cornstarch

3 tbsp cool water

1 large egg, beaten

½ tsp toasted sesame oil

PLANT-BASED OPTION

Egg → 3 tbsp plant-based egg mixture (or omit)

1. In a medium stock pot or Dutch oven, heat the cooking oil on medium-high heat until it shimmers. Add the mushrooms and sauté, tossing frequently, until browned, about 3 minutes. Add the white scallions and ginger and sauté for 1 minute.

2. Stir in the stock, tofu, bamboo shoots, rice vinegar, soy sauce, brown sugar, pepper, and chili paste. Reduce the heat to medium-low and simmer for 10 minutes, stirring occasionally.

3. In a small bowl, mix the cornstarch with the cool water to form into a slurry. Pour into the pot and stir until thickened. (Make a little more slurry if you prefer a thicker soup.) Drizzle in the egg until ribbons form.

4. Ladle into soup bowls, drizzle with sesame oil, and garnish with green scallions.

PUMPKIN, CORN & WHITE FISH CONGEE

Inspired by home

♫ *Come Together – Scary Pockets and Mario Jose*

SERVES 4 TO 6 🦐 🌱 🐟

Congee is classic Chinese comfort food. It serves as a reliable breakfast staple, a canvas to unleash your fridge-cleaning skills, and a nourishing alternative to chicken soup when you're sick. Whenever I dig into a steaming bowl of congee, memories flood in from meals at flashy dim sum palaces and our family's go-to, Congee Queen, a beloved Toronto chain serving up Cantonese eats late into the night. Congee itself is naturally gluten-free, but it's commonly served with gluten-filled toppings such as pork floss, soy-marinated tofu, or yau ja gwai (a Chinese deep-fried doughnut). This version, with soft pumpkin and sweet corn, is similar to the congee found at dim sum restaurants, but with white fish for added protein, if you're feeling it. It is my childhood in a bowl, serving as a forever source of comfort.

1 cup jasmine rice, rinsed

12 cups water

1-inch knob ginger, julienned

1½ tsp kosher salt, plus more to taste

1 tbsp GF miso paste

2 cups pumpkin or kabocha squash, peeled and cut into ½-inch cubes

2 scallions, green part only, cut into 2-inch segments and thinly sliced lengthwise

1 cup corn kernels (about 1 cob)

1 tbsp unsalted cooking wine or sake

1 tsp rice vinegar

1 lb (450 g) skinless white fish fillets (such as basa, cod, or haddock), cut into bite-sized pieces (optional)

OPTIONAL GARNISHES
A drizzle of GF chili oil (such as chili crisp)

Fresh cilantro, chopped

GF fried garlic

Toasted peanuts (see page 25)

PLANT-BASED OPTION
Omit the fish

1. In a large stock pot or Dutch oven, combine the rice, 10 cups of the water, ginger, salt, and miso. Bring to a boil, then reduce the heat to medium, maintaining consistent large bubbles so that the rice grains toss around in the pot and don't sink and stick to the bottom. Cover, leaving the lid ajar, and simmer for 25 minutes, stirring frequently, until thickened into a porridge.

2. Add the pumpkin and the remaining water and simmer, uncovered, for 20 minutes, stirring occasionally and scraping up any bits stuck to the bottom. Whisk to break up the rice grains. Stir in the scallions, corn, cooking wine, and rice vinegar, and adjust the salt to taste. For added protein, if using, add the fish and simmer for 3 minutes, until opaque.

3. Ladle into soup bowls and garnish as desired with chili oil, cilantro, fried garlic, and peanuts.

PEANUTTY RAINBOW CHARD & SWEET POTATO CHOWDER

SERVES 4

Inspired by the restaurant
Thaïlande in Montreal

♫ *Left Hand Free – Alt-J*

This recipe came about when I was craving the flavors of Panang curry but wanted the slurpability of soup. Like the curry, this chowder is peanutty and fragrant from makrut lime leaves, making it simultaneously rich and bright—a quality I strive for in all of my food. Sweet potatoes make up the bulk of the soup and add a delicate sweetness, while the rainbow chard brings pops of green, pink, and yellow throughout. The result is hearty and vibrant—a great pick-me-up when you need a lift.

2 tbsp neutral high-heat cooking oil

2 cloves garlic, minced

1 yellow onion, diced

1 jalapeño, minced (keep the seeds for extra spice)

2 large sweet potatoes, peeled and diced

2 cups unsalted chicken stock, vegetable stock, or Freezer Bag Stock (page 24)

1 can (14 oz/400 ml) full-fat coconut milk

1 can (28 oz/796 ml) diced tomatoes, with juice

1 tsp kosher salt

1 tbsp Thai red curry paste

½ cup chunky peanut butter, or ¼ cup smooth peanut butter + ¼ cup chopped peanuts

4 to 6 stalks rainbow chard, shredded

Fresh cilantro and/or scallions, chopped (optional)

½ lime, cut into wedges

PLANT-BASED NOTE
Check for seafood products in the curry paste

1. In a medium stock pot or Dutch oven, heat the oil on medium heat until it shimmers. Add the garlic, onions, and jalapeños and sauté for 2 minutes or until fragrant. Add the sweet potatoes and sauté for 2 to 3 minutes, until just starting to soften.

2. Stir in the stock, coconut milk, tomatoes, salt, and curry paste. Bring to a boil, then reduce the heat to low and simmer for 12 to 15 minutes, stirring occasionally, until the sweet potatoes are fork-tender. Turn off the heat.

3. Using an immersion blender in the pot, blend the soup until just thickened and chunky. (Or ladle half of the soup into a stand blender and blend, leaving it thick and chunky, then return the soup to the pot.)

4. Return the soup to low heat. Stir in the peanut butter and chard and simmer for 5 to 6 minutes, stirring a few times, until the liquid has reduced slightly and the chard is tender.

5. Ladle into soup bowls and garnish with cilantro (if using) and lime wedges.

NOTE
For peanut allergies, use an alternative nut butter or tahini instead of peanut butter.

NICE WITH RICE

I often find myself wondering how many grains of rice I've eaten in my life, 'cause let me tell ya, it's A LOT. We had rice every night of the week when I was growing up, with generations of rice cookers standing proudly beside us at every moment. My grandpa would buy rice by the 18-pound bag, refilling the giant plastic tub we kept under our kitchen sink for many years. I've watched my family measure, pour, wash, and swirl rice time and time again, the sounds of this ritual forever etched into my memory.

Rice has been a source of nourishment for Asian populations for centuries, and it remains a saving grace for those on gluten-free diets. There's something so alluring about a simple bowl of plain white rice, filling the air with its nutty and mildly sweet perfume. Its ability to soak up sauces is truly a gift, making it the perfect canvas for deeply flavorful stews. It will always be a reliable source of sustenance and a beloved part of our home.

Although many other recipes in this book also pair well with rice, this chapter is all about saucy dishes made in woks, stockpots, or Dutch ovens that come alive when paired with rice, like my remixed classic Tomato, Egg & Pesto Stir-Fry (page 121) and hearty Vietnamese Short Rib Stew (page 101). They stray from sneaky flour-based roux to thicken them, instead using a gluten-free slurry or ingredients that naturally release starch. As these dishes make for excellent leftovers, you'll want to steam them properly when reheating—see the sidebar on page 8 for guidance.

While you can use your preferred rice variety, I typically cook jasmine or short-grain white rice for these dishes—the recipe on page 24 will help you make perfect steamed rice.

Scan me to
listen along!

MASSAMAN BEEF CURRY
with Baby Potatoes

Inspired by the restaurant PAI in Toronto

♫ *Could I Be – Sylvan Esso*

SERVES 4 TO 6

Massaman is hands down my favorite curry. And I'm the type of person who finds it hard to pick favorites. Add coconut milk, a handful of concentrated spices, plus a couple of hours of slow simmering, and it transforms into a luscious, multidimensional curry with tender, melty beef (made all the more tender and flavorful by salting ahead of time—make sure to leave time for this!). The addition of baby potatoes at the end naturally thickens the stew.

2 lb (900 g) beef chuck, cut into 1½-inch cubes

½ tsp kosher salt

1 can (14 oz/400 ml) full-fat coconut milk, unshaken (see note on page 13)

1 tbsp neutral high-heat cooking oil

½ cup massaman or yellow curry paste (see curry paste on page 14)

3 cardamom pods

2 star anise pods

1 cinnamon stick

1 bay leaf

1 yellow onion, sliced into thick chunks

1 lb (450 g) baby potatoes, halved

¼ cup toasted peanuts (see page 25) or chunky peanut butter (for a creamier stew)

2 tbsp brown sugar or maple syrup

2 tbsp GF fish sauce

2 tbsp lime juice (about 1 lime)

4 sprigs fresh cilantro and/or basil (Thai or Italian), chopped (optional)

Steamed rice (see page 24), for serving

1. In a large bowl, coat the beef with the salt (to draw out the moisture), cover, and refrigerate. Leave this to marinate while the oven is preheating, or for a more flavorful stew, do this for at least 2 hours or up to 24 hours.

2. Preheat the oven to 275°F (135°C). Pat the beef dry with paper towel.

3. Remove ¼ cup of cream from the top of the can of coconut milk..In a Dutch oven or ovenproof pot, heat the coconut cream and oil on medium heat. Add the curry paste and cook, stirring, for 2 minutes, until fragrant.

4. Stir in the remaining coconut cream, coconut milk, beef, and enough water to just cover the meat (about 1 cup). Place the cardamom, star anise, cinnamon, and bay leaf in a paper tea bag to make a spice packet and add to the pot (or add them loose). Bring to a boil, then turn off the heat.

5. Cover the pot, leaving the lid ajar, and transfer it to the oven. Cook for 2 to 2½ hours, until the beef is fork-tender.

6. Return the pot to the stovetop on low heat and skim off excess fat (see note). Add the onions, potatoes, peanuts, brown sugar, and fish sauce, cover, and simmer for 15 minutes, stirring occasionally. Turn off the heat, discard the spice packet, and stir in the lime juice.

7. Ladle into bowls (avoiding the whole spices if they were added loose) and garnish with cilantro (if using). Serve with steamed rice.

NOTES

For a stovetop pressure cooker or Instant Pot: Use Sauté mode on high for step 3, then pressure-cook the beef in the spiced coconut mixture for 30 minutes, with a quick release. Add remaining ingredients and simmer on Sauté on low heat for 15 minutes, stirring occasionally.

After braising and before serving, skim excess fat into an empty can with a large spoon or ladle and dispose of it once it has cooled. Place the can in the fridge to speed up the process.

SPICY KOREAN-STYLE SEAFOOD STEW

Inspired by
jjampong and bouillabaisse

♫ *Out of Love (feat. Macy Gray)*
– Busty and the Bass

SERVES 4 🦐 🌿

In high school, I loved eating out with friends at Korean spots in North Toronto—affordable, exciting, with sizzling plates and bubbling stews served with rice and pickled sides. This stew blends my love of Korean food with my French culinary training, featuring a fiery broth, fresh seafood, baby potatoes, spinach, cilantro, and toasted mustard seeds. It's also delicious with gluten-free spaghetti or toasted gluten-free bread.

1 lb (450 g) live mussels or clams

2 tbsp neutral high-heat cooking oil

4 anchovy fillets

4 cloves garlic, minced

1 yellow onion, sliced

2-inch knob ginger, minced

¼ cup dry white wine or unsalted cooking wine or sake

4 cups unsalted chicken stock, vegetable stock, or Freezer Bag Stock (page 24)

8 oz (225 g) baby potatoes, halved

1 tbsp GF miso paste

1 tbsp GF fish sauce

1 tbsp maple syrup

1½ tsp mild paprika

1 tsp unsalted Korean chili flakes (gochugaru) or Kashmiri chili powder

2 tsp toasted sesame oil

½ lemon

2 cups baby spinach (about 4 oz/115 g)

12 oz (340 g) large or jumbo shrimp, peeled and deveined (see note on page 83)

12 oz (340 g) skinless flaky white fish fillets (such as cod), cut into 2-inch squares

Fresh cilantro, chopped (optional)

1 tbsp toasted mustard seeds

Steamed rice (see page 24), for serving

SUB
If you can't find gochugaru or Kashmiri chili powder, use ¾ tsp mild paprika + ¼ tsp cayenne.

1. Place the mussels in a large bowl of cold water and rinse off any debris, then drain in a colander. Using a paper towel, pull off any beards. Squeeze the mussels shut; if any stay open, discard them.

2. In a medium stock pot or Dutch oven, heat the cooking oil on medium heat until it shimmers. Reduce the heat to medium-low. Add the anchovies, garlic, onions, and ginger and sauté until fragrant, about 3 to 4 minutes. Add the wine to deglaze the pot, using a wooden spoon to scrape off any browned bits (called fond), until the liquid has evaporated, about 1 to 2 minutes.

3. Stir in the stock, potatoes, miso, fish sauce, maple syrup, paprika, chili flakes, sesame oil, and lemon. Bring to a boil, then reduce the heat and simmer for 12 to 15 minutes, stirring occasionally, until the potatoes are fork-tender and the broth becomes a gorgeous scarlet color.

4. Add the spinach and the mussels and simmer for 2 minutes. Then, add the shrimp and cod, cover, and continue simmering for another 3 minutes, until the mussels have opened, the shrimp turns pink and firm, and the cod is opaque. Discard any mussels that did not open. Discard the lemon.

5. Ladle into pasta bowls and garnish with cilantro (if using) and mustard seeds. Serve with steamed rice.

NOTE
For a plant-based version, try White Bean Stew with Kimchi & Yu Choy (page 118).

VIETNAMESE SHORT RIB STEW

Inspired by bò kho

♫ *Henny & Gingerale – Mayer Hawthorne*

SERVES 4 TO 6

When I crave something richer at a pho restaurant, I order bò kho—a deeply flavored beef stew with pho spices plus garlic, lemongrass, tomatoes, and chilies. Typically served with rice noodles, this version has a concentrated sauce with melt-in-your-mouth carrots and parsnips over rice. I like my root vegetables fully cooked—it's all or nothing for me.

4 lb (1.8 kg) thick-cut beef short ribs or oxtail

1 tsp kosher salt

2 tbsp neutral high-heat cooking oil

2 stalks lemongrass, cut into 2-inch-long segments (see note)

2 carrots, cut on a diagonal into 1-inch chunks

2 parsnips, cut on a diagonal into 1-inch chunks

1 yellow onion, thinly sliced

1 head garlic, cloves minced

1-inch knob ginger, minced

¼ cup dry red or white wine

2 cups coconut water

1 cup unsalted chicken stock, beef stock, or Freezer Bag Stock (page 24)

¼ cup tomato paste

1 tbsp mild paprika

2 tsp Chinese five-spice powder, or 1 tsp ground cinnamon + 1 tsp ground cloves

2 tsp brown sugar or maple syrup

½ tsp unsalted Korean chili flakes (gochugaru) or Kashmiri chili powder

2 tbsp GF fish sauce

2 tbsp GF soy sauce or tamari

Fresh cilantro, basil (Thai or Italian), and/or scallions, chopped

GF fried garlic (optional)

Steamed rice (see page 24), for serving

SUB

If you can't find gochugaru or Kashmiri chili powder, use ½ tsp mild paprika + ⅛ tsp cayenne.

1. In a large bowl, coat the short ribs with salt (to draw out the moisture), cover, and refrigerate. Leave this to marinate while the oven is preheating, or for a more flavorful stew, do this for at least 2 hours or up to 24 hours.

2. Preheat the oven to 275°F (135°C). Pat the short ribs dry with paper towel.

3. In a Dutch oven or ovenproof pot, heat the oil on medium-high heat until it shimmers. Working in batches, sear the short ribs until nicely browned, about 2 to 3 minutes per side. Transfer to a bowl and drain off all but 2 tablespoons of fat.

4. Add the lemongrass, carrots, parsnips, and onions to the pot and sauté for 3 minutes. Add the garlic and ginger and sauté for 1 minute. Add the wine to deglaze the pot, scraping up any browned bits (called fond) with a wooden spoon, until the liquid has evaporated.

5. Return the short ribs and any juices to the pot and stir in the coconut water, stock, tomato paste, paprika, five-spice powder, brown sugar, chili flakes, fish sauce, and soy sauce. Bring to a boil, then turn off the heat.

6. Cover the pot, leaving the lid ajar, and transfer it to the oven. Cook for 2½ to 3 hours, until the short ribs are melty tender.

7. Return the pot to the stovetop and skim off excess fat (see note on page 97).

8. Ladle into bowls and garnish with cilantro and fried garlic (if using). Serve with steamed rice.

NOTES

If you can't find lemongrass, stir in 2 tsp lemon zest after skimming off the fat in step 7.

You can use a stovetop pressure cooker or Instant Pot instead: sear in the pressure cooker or on the Sauté mode of an Instant Pot, then pressure-cook for 45 minutes, followed by a quick pressure release.

GOCHUJANG-BRAISED PORK SHOULDER & FIXINGS

Inspired by bossam

♫ *Feel Your Weight (Poolside Remix) – Rhye*

SERVES 4

This gochujang-braised pork shoulder is all about embracing the joy of good food and gathering with your favorite peeps, something that non-allergy folks can take for granted. Gochujang can be made with or without wheat, so it's tricky to guarantee you're getting it gluten-free when dining out. This recipe is the weekend dinner party version of my Laotian-Style Lettuce Wraps (page 138), featuring fiery, slow-cooked pork shoulder served with crisp lettuce, snackable seaweed, steamed rice, GF kimchi, and pickled onions. It's a lively, interactive meal that you can easily scale up for larger crews.

2 lb (900 g) pork shoulder, trimmed and cut into 1-inch-thick slabs

½ tsp kosher salt

2 anchovy fillets

2 cloves garlic, sliced

1 Asian pear or sweet apple (such as Fuji, Ambrosia, or Gala), peeled and cut into cubes

1-inch knob ginger, sliced

2 tbsp GF gochujang (Korean chili paste)

2 tbsp GF soy sauce or tamari

1 tbsp rice vinegar

½ tbsp toasted sesame oil

1 tbsp neutral high-heat cooking oil

¼ cup dry white wine or unsalted cooking wine or sake

TO SERVE

1 bunch Bibb or butter lettuce, torn into individual leaves

2 packets (0.17 oz/5 g each) seaweed

A large handful of fresh cilantro and/or shiso leaves

GF kimchi

Pickled Red Onions (page 25) or Quick Pickled Red Onions (page 25)

Ssamjang (page 30)

Steamed rice (see page 24), for serving

SUB

If you can't find GF gochujang, use 1 tbsp GF miso paste + 1 tbsp chili paste (such as sambal oelek or Calabrian) + 1 tsp maple syrup.

1. In a large bowl, coat the pork with salt (to draw out the moisture), cover, and refrigerate. Leave this to marinate while the oven is preheating, or for a more flavorful stew, do this for at least 2 hours or up to 24 hours.

2. Preheat the oven to 275°F (135°C). Pat the pork dry with paper towel.

3. In a blender, combine the anchovies, garlic, Asian pears, ginger, gochujang, soy sauce, rice vinegar, and sesame oil. Blend until well combined.

4. In a Dutch oven or ovenproof pot, heat the cooking oil on medium-high heat until it shimmers. Add the pork, making sure there's plenty of room between pieces (sear in batches if it doesn't all fit). Sear until nicely browned, about 2 to 3 minutes per side. Return all pork to the pan (if you seared in batches). Add the wine to deglaze the bottom of the pot, scraping up the fond (any browned bits) with a wooden spoon, until the liquid has evaporated. Stir in the anchovy mixture and bring to a boil, then turn off the heat.

5. Cover the pot, leaving the lid ajar, and transfer it to the oven. Cook for 2 hours or until the pork shoulder is fork-tender.

6. Return the pot to the stovetop and skim off excess fat (see note on page 97). Using two forks, shred the pork in the pot.

7. Transfer the pork mixture to a large serving bowl. Arrange the lettuce, seaweed, and cilantro on a platter. Place the kimchi, pickled onions, and Ssamjang in separate small bowls. Serve everything family-style, with steamed rice.

NOTES

You can use a stovetop pressure cooker or Instant Pot instead: sear in the pressure cooker or on the Sauté mode of an Instant Pot, then pressure-cook for 40 minutes, followed by a quick pressure release. Stir in the cannellini beans and simmer, uncovered, on Sauté mode on low heat for 15 minutes, stirring occasionally.

TOMATOEY MUSSELS
with Chinese Sausage

Inspired by nam prik ong,
a Thai pork and tomato dip

♫ *Heavy, California – Jungle*

SERVES 4

If you're a saucy person, mussels are awesome for dunking in delicious sauce! Once you polish off your first mussel, you can use the shell to pinch the meat out of the others. It's a hands-on experience that brings you fully into the food, allowing minimal distraction from the outside world. This dish is inspired by a Thai pork and tomato dip that is usually served with shrimp chips and raw veggies as a snack.

4 lb (1.8 kg) live mussels

1 tbsp neutral high-heat cooking oil

8 sprigs fresh cilantro, leaves and stems separated, chopped

4 anchovy fillets

4 cloves garlic, minced

2 small shallots, minced (about ¼ cup)

½ tsp unsalted Korean chili flakes (gochugaru) or Kashmiri chili powder

4 links GF Chinese sausage (lap cheong) or 4 slices maple-flavored bacon, diced

4 tomatoes, cut into wedges

1 cup dry white wine

½ cup unsalted chicken stock, vegetable stock, or Freezer Bag Stock (page 24)

2 tsp maple syrup

Fresh cilantro leaves, to garnish

Steamed rice (see page 24), for serving

SUB
If you can't find gochugaru or Kashmiri chili powder, use ½ tsp mild paprika + ⅛ tsp cayenne.

1. Place the mussels in a large bowl of cold water and rinse off any debris, then drain in a colander. Using a paper towel, pull off any beards. Squeeze the mussels shut; if any stay open, discard them.

2. In a medium stock pot or Dutch oven, heat the oil on medium heat until it shimmers. Add the cilantro stems, anchovies, garlic, shallots, and chili flakes and sauté for 2 minutes or until fragrant. Add the sausages and sauté for 3 minutes or until just crispy on the edges. (If using bacon, fry until crispy, about 5 to 6 minutes.)

3. Add the tomatoes, increase the heat to medium-high, and sauté until the tomatoes are sizzling. Reduce the heat to medium and simmer for 10 minutes, stirring occasionally, until the tomatoes are jammy and just starting to stick to the bottom of the pot. Add the wine and cook, scraping up any browned bits (called fond), for 3 to 4 minutes, until most of the wine has evaporated.

4. Stir in the stock and maple syrup. Increase the heat to high, add the mussels, cover, and cook for 5 minutes or until the mussels have opened. Discard any mussels that did not open.

5. Ladle into bowls and garnish with cilantro. Serve with steamed rice.

NOTE
If you can't find Chinese sausage, maple bacon or any kind of sweet sausage are great substitutes to build flavor and round out the tart tomatoes.

CANTO-STYLE MAPO TOFU

SERVES 4 TO 6 🐟 🌱 🍃

Inspired by the Scarborough
mom-and-pop gems

♫ *Crazy – Gnarls Barkley*

Growing up, I didn't understand why many of my friends were not fans of tofu. To me, it was the perfect vessel for soaking up the sauciest flavor bombs, turning any bowl of rice into the ultimate comfort food. This particular dish changed the game for Reid, with his gluten intolerance (and skepticism of tofu), and quickly became a household staple for us. For those familiar with mapo tofu, this recipe is closer to the Cantonese version I grew up eating, which is less spicy than its original Sichuanese relative with tongue-numbing Sichuan peppercorns.

14 oz (400 g) soft or medium tofu, cubed

2 tsp GF miso paste

1 tsp tamari or GF soy sauce

1 tsp chili paste (such as sambal oelek or Calabrian)

4 pitted kalamata olives, chopped

1 tbsp neutral high-heat cooking oil

5 oz (150 g) lean or medium ground pork

2 cloves garlic, minced

1-inch knob ginger, minced

½ cup unsalted chicken stock, vegetable stock, or Freezer Bag Stock (page 24)

¼ tsp freshly cracked white or black pepper

2 tsp cornstarch

2 tsp cool water

Kosher salt to taste

Fresh cilantro and/or scallions, chopped (optional)

Toasted Sichuan peppercorns, freshly cracked (optional)

GF chili oil (such as chili crisp) to taste (optional)

Steamed rice (see page 24), for serving

PLANT-BASED/PESCATARIAN OPTION

Ground pork → plant-based ground round (such as Beyond or Impossible) or minced cremini mushrooms

1. Bring a medium saucepan of salted water to a boil. Turn off the heat but leave the pan on the element. Add the tofu and let it hang out in this jacuzzi bath.

2. In a small bowl, mix together the miso, tamari, chili paste, and olives.

3. In another medium saucepan or a wok, heat the oil on medium heat until it shimmers. Add the miso mixture and pork and sauté for 3 to 5 minutes, breaking the pork up with a wooden spoon, until browned. Add the garlic and ginger and sauté for 1 minute.

4. Using a slotted spoon, remove the tofu from the hot water bath and gently transfer it to the pan or wok. Use the back of a wooden spoon or rubber spatula to gently push the tofu around, coating the tofu in sauce. Avoid breaking it and do not stir aggressively. Add the stock and pepper. Let it come to a bubble, then reduce the heat to a simmer.

5. In a small bowl, mix the cornstarch with the cool water to make a slurry. Pour into the pan and simmer, mixing gently and shaking the pan, until the liquid thickens and clings to the tofu. (Make a little more slurry if you prefer a thicker sauce.) Season with salt.

6. Ladle into bowls and garnish with cilantro (if using). For a tongue-numbing experience, sprinkle with peppercorns. If using, drizzle with chili oil. Serve with steamed rice.

NOTE

It can be hard to find gluten-free chili bean paste (doubanjiang), which is traditionally in mapo tofu, but the mixture of GF miso paste, tamari, chili paste, and chopped kalamata olives offers a similar flavor profile.

KING OYSTER MUSHROOMS, PLANTAINS & GAI LAN CURRY

Inspired by the tropical flavors
I keep coming back to
♫ *Yes, No, Maybe – Dam Swindle,
Tom Misch, and Lorenz Rhode*

SERVES 4

As a meat eater who's just as happy eating vegetables, I wanted to create a deeply savory plant-based dish fit for a weeknight meal. In this recipe, caramelized plantains and robust king oyster mushrooms braise in an aromatic coconut sauce until it thickens into a spoonable gravy. Throw in gai lan (Chinese broccoli) at the last minute for crunch and color contrast. It's a hearty dish not particularly rooted in any cuisine, but it has elements of the tropics, which inspire me daily, especially during the winter months in Canada.

4 cloves garlic, sliced

2 small shallots, sliced (about ¼ cup)

1-inch knob ginger, sliced

1 can full-fat coconut milk

1 tbsp neutral high-heat cooking oil

2 fully ripe plantains, or 3 green bananas, sliced into thick diagonal slices

10½ oz (300 g) king oyster mushrooms, halved lengthwise and cut into large chunks

1 stalk lemongrass, white part only, smashed (see note)

¼ cup unsweetened coconut flakes

3 tbsp GF soy sauce or tamari

1 tbsp rice vinegar

1 tbsp maple syrup

½ tbsp chili paste (such as sambal oelek or Calabrian)

1 tsp freshly cracked black pepper

⅛ tsp ground turmeric

8 stalks baby gai lan, stems and leaves separated and cut into 1-inch sections

Fresh cilantro, chopped (optional)

Steamed rice (see page 24), for serving

1. Using an immersion blender, stand blender, or mortar and pestle, pulverize the garlic, shallots, ginger, and coconut milk until uniform in consistency.

2. In a large nonstick frying pan or wok, heat the oil on medium heat until it shimmers. Add the plantains and fry for 2 to 3 minutes per side, flipping delicately, until nicely browned and caramelized.

3. Stir in the coconut milk mixture, mushrooms, lemongrass, coconut, soy sauce, rice vinegar, maple syrup, chili paste, pepper, and turmeric. Reduce the heat to medium-low and simmer for 15 minutes, stirring occasionally, until the mushrooms have absorbed the sauce. Add the gai lan and simmer for 5 minutes, stirring a few times.

4. Ladle into bowls and garnish with cilantro (if using). Serve with steamed rice.

NOTE
Use the dull edge of a chef's knife or a rolling pin to smash the lemongrass. If you can't find lemongrass, stir in 1 tsp lemon zest at the end of step 3.

VIBRANT GREEN CURRY

SERVES 4 TO 6 🌶 🌱 🍃

Inspired by a short stint at a smoothie start-up

♫ *Sprawl II (Mountains Beyond Mountains) – Arcade Fire*

I wanted a way to make my green curries more vibrant in color, then I thought, why not blend kale into my coconut milk, just like I used to with the smoothies at my day job? The result makes for an extremely lively-looking curry, with extra vitamins and fiber to boot! Feel free to throw in any crisp green vegetables, like green beans, sugar snap peas, snow peas, or broccoli, that you have in your fridge.

1 can (14 oz/400 ml) full-fat coconut milk

1 leaf lacinato or curly kale, thick stem removed, chopped

1 tbsp neutral high-heat cooking oil

2 to 3 tbsp Thai green curry paste

8 oz (225 g) butternut squash, peeled and cut into 1-inch cubes

8 oz (225 g) GF fried tofu or firm tofu, cubed

4 makrut lime leaves, crumbled (see note)

1 yellow onion, cut into large wedges

½ cup unsalted chicken stock,vegetable stock, or Freezer Bag Stock (page 24)

1 tbsp brown sugar or maple syrup

2 tbsp GF fish sauce

8 oz (225 g) large or jumbo shrimp, peeled and deveined (see note on page 83)

1 red, yellow, or orange bell pepper, cut into strips and halved

½ lime, cut into wedges

Fresh cilantro and/or basil (Thai or Italian), chopped (optional)

¼ cup toasted peanuts (see page 25) (optional)

GF fried shallots or garlic (optional)

Steamed rice (see page 24), for serving

PLANT-BASED OPTION

- Shrimp → hearty mushrooms (such as shiitake, king oyster, chanterelle, or lobster), stems removed, if needed and kept whole (see note)
- Fish sauce → GF soy sauce or tamari

1. In a blender, blend the coconut milk and kale until the kale is fully incorporated and the mixture is vibrant green.

2. In a medium saucepan or wok, heat the oil on medium heat until it shimmers. Add 2 tablespoons of the curry paste and cook, stirring, for 1 to 2 minutes. Carefully pour in the coconut milk mixture.

3. Stir in the squash, tofu, lime leaves, onions, stock, brown sugar, and fish sauce. Bring to a boil, then reduce the heat to medium-low and simmer for 8 to 10 minutes, stirring occasionally, until the squash is tender. Taste the curry and, if using, add the remaining curry paste for more kick.

4. Add the shrimp and bell peppers and simmer for 2 to 3 minutes, until the shrimp is pink, firm, and opaque and the peppers are crisp-tender.

5. Ladle into bowls and garnish with lime wedges and, if using, cilantro, peanuts, and fried shallots. Serve with steamed rice.

NOTES

If using mushrooms instead of shrimp, sauté them in the pan until browned before adding the curry paste.

You can use a large sweet potato in place of the butternut squash, but increase the simmering time in step 3 to 15 to 20 minutes, until the sweet potato is tender.

If you can't find lime leaves, stir in 2 tsp lime zest at the end of step 4.

JAPANESE-STYLE CURRY

SERVES 4 🔥 🌱 🍃

Inspired by Curry House visits with my sisters in LA

♫ *Fortress – Pinback*

If you have a gluten allergy, you've probably never had a Japanese curry, since it's usually made with a flour-based roux. It's velvety and mildly spiced, great on top of Chicken Thigh Katsu (page 152). With origins in India, curry was introduced to Japan by the British and promptly became a national dish that stands as its own. It's a fascinating blend of Indian ingredients, Western techniques, and a Japanese palate, showcasing the complexity of culinary fusion that is always present in the foods we eat. All we have to do is dig a little deeper to uncover the rich narratives behind them.

1 tbsp neutral high-heat cooking oil

2 carrots, sliced into rounds or half moons

1 yellow onion, diced

4 cups water

4 tsp GF miso paste

1 large or 2 medium Yukon gold potatoes, cut into cubes

2 tbsp unsalted butter

1-inch knob ginger, minced

2 tbsp GF all-purpose flour

1½ tbsp curry powder

½ tsp unsalted Korean chili flakes (gochugaru) or Kashmiri chili powder

1 tbsp ketchup

1 lb (227 g) boneless skinless chicken thighs, cut into 1-inch cubes

½ cup frozen or fresh green peas

1 tsp rice vinegar

Kosher salt to taste

A few scallions, chopped

Steamed rice (see page 24), for serving

DAIRY-FREE/PLANT-BASED/PESCATARIAN OPTION

- Butter → plant-based butter or neutral high-heat cooking oil
- Plant-based/pescatarian: Chicken thighs → 2 cans (14 oz/398 ml each) chickpeas, drained and rinsed (about 3 cups)

SUB

If you can't find gochugaru or Kashmiri chili powder, use ½ tsp mild paprika + ⅛ tsp cayenne.

1. In a medium saucepan or wok, heat the oil on medium-high heat until it shimmers. Add the carrots and onions and sauté for 1 to 2 minutes, until just softened. Reduce the heat to medium-low and cook, stirring occasionally, for 8 to 9 minutes, until the onions are translucent and the carrots have just softened.

2. Stir in the water, miso, and potatoes. Reduce the heat to low, cover, and simmer for 15 minutes, stirring occasionally.

3. Meanwhile, in a small frying pan, melt the butter on medium-low heat. Add the ginger and sauté until aromatic, about 1 minute. Stir in the flour, curry powder, and chili flakes until a thick paste forms.

4. Add the curry roux and ketchup to the saucepan and stir until well combined. Stir in the chicken and simmer, uncovered, for 5 to 6 minutes, continuing to stir, until the curry has thickened and the chicken is no longer pink inside. Stir in the peas and cook for 1 minute. Turn off the heat, stir in the rice vinegar and season with salt.

5. Ladle into bowls and garnish with scallions. Serve with steamed rice.

NOTE

This curry sauce is perfect to ladle over the Chicken Thigh Katsu (page 152); just reduce the water to 2 cups and the miso paste to 2 teaspoons. In step 4, after stirring in the roux and ketchup, go straight to stirring in the peas.

ROASTED COCONUT TAMARI CHICKEN

Inspired by Filipino adobo

♫ *Fader – The Temper Trap*

SERVES 4

Those who have eaten with me know that I look for balance in every meal. If a dish is overly rich, I instinctively reach for something tart and puckery. If a dish is too salty, I counteract it with refreshing bites of something fresh. A great meal is a well-balanced one, and this dish is an example of simple food done well. Inspired by Filipino adobo, this rendition is wonderfully tangy from rice vinegar, savory from tamari (gluten-free, of course!), and rich from the coconut milk—a saucy addition to your weeknight rotation. Serve with simple blanched greens as the final touch to a perfectly balanced plate of comforting flavors.

¾ cup full-fat coconut milk

⅓ cup GF tamari or soy sauce

¼ cup rice vinegar

1 tsp whole black peppercorns

3 bay leaves

4 cloves garlic, smashed with the blade of a knife

1 long red Thai chili, thinly sliced, or 2 tsp chili paste (such as sambal oelek or Calabrian)

1-inch piece turmeric root, sliced, or ¼ tsp ground turmeric

1-inch knob ginger, sliced

4 bone-in, skin-on chicken legs, thigh and drumstick separated

Steamed rice (see page 24), for serving

1. Preheat the oven to 425°F (220°C).

2. In a Dutch oven or ovenproof pot, combine the coconut milk, tamari, rice vinegar, peppercorns, bay leaves, garlic, chilies, turmeric, and ginger. Lay the chicken, skin side up, flat in the pot, making sure the liquid covers it three-quarters of the way up. If it doesn't, add up to ½ cup water. Bring the sauce to a boil over high heat.

3. Transfer the pot to the oven and cook, uncovered, for 40 minutes or until the chicken is browned and tender. Spoon the sauce over top. Discard the bay leaves.

4. Portion the chicken onto plates and ladle sauce over top. Serve with steamed rice.

ROASTED SICHUAN-STYLE EGGPLANT

with Ground Pork

Inspired by
fish-fragrant eggplant

♫ *Waterfalls – TLC*

SERVES 2

For a long time, this childhood staple felt difficult to recreate, since it usually involves deep-frying the eggplant before stir-frying, to soften it and help it absorb flavor. I wanted to find an at-home-friendly way of achieving this dish, so roasting the eggplant in the oven became my go-to method. While it does require the extra step of roasting, the advantage is that you can avoid the messy splatter of frying with excessive oil.

2 Asian eggplants, ends cut off, quartered lengthwise and cut into 3-inch sections

1 tsp kosher salt

2 tbsp neutral high-heat cooking oil

4 oz (115 g) lean or medium ground pork

2 cloves garlic, minced

2 scallions, white and green parts separated, chopped

1-inch knob ginger, minced

1 cup unsalted chicken stock, vegetable stock, or Freezer Bag Stock (page 24)

1 tbsp GF soy sauce or tamari

1 tbsp GF Chinese black vinegar (or see page 13 for sub)

½ tbsp chili paste (such as sambal oelek or Calabrian)

2 tsp maple syrup

2 tsp cornstarch

2 tsp cool water

Fresh cilantro, chopped

Steamed rice (see page 24), for serving

PLANT-BASED/PESCATARIAN OPTION

Ground pork → plant-based ground round (such as Beyond or Impossible) or minced cremini mushrooms

1. Place the eggplants in a colander in the sink and toss them with the salt. Set aside while the oven is preheating.

2. Preheat the oven to 425°F (220°C). Line a baking sheet with parchment paper.

3. Transfer the eggplant to a large bowl, and toss with 1 tablespoon of the oil. Spread out in a single layer on the prepared pan. Roast for 20 to 25 minutes, tossing halfway through, until tender and golden along the edges.

4. In a large nonstick frying pan or wok, heat the remaining oil on medium-high heat until it shimmers. Add the pork and sauté for 3 to 4 minutes, breaking it up with a wooden spoon, until browned. Add the garlic, white scallions, and ginger and sauté for 1 minute.

5. Stir in the stock, soy sauce, vinegar, chili paste, and maple syrup. Add the roasted eggplant, reduce the heat to medium, and simmer for 5 minutes, stirring occasionally.

6. In a small bowl, mix the cornstarch with the cool water to make a slurry. Pour into the pan and simmer for 2 minutes to thicken.

7. Ladle into bowls and garnish with the green scallions and cilantro. Serve with steamed rice.

NOTE

This recipe works best with small or skinny eggplants, as they contain fewer seeds and their skins are more tender. Salting the eggplants helps to draw out excess moisture, allowing them to absorb the sharp and mouthwatering sauce.

WHITE BEAN STEW
with Kimchi & Yu Choy

Inspired by Korean tofu stew
(sundubu jjigae)

♫ *Doo Wop (That Thing)*
– Lauryn Hill

SERVES 2 TO 4

1 tbsp neutral high-heat cooking oil

2 slices bacon, thinly sliced
widthwise, or 1 to 2 GF sausages,
sliced into medallions

4 oz (115 g) cremini mushrooms,
stems removed and caps thinly
sliced

6 cloves garlic, minced

½ yellow onion, diced

2 tbsp dry white wine or unsalted
cooking wine or sake

1½ cups water

½ cup GF kimchi, chopped

1 can (19 oz/540 ml) cannellini beans

1 tbsp brown sugar or maple syrup

½ tbsp GF miso paste

1 tsp unsalted Korean chili flakes
(gochugaru) or Kashmiri chili
powder

1 tsp GF fish sauce

1 tsp toasted sesame oil

8 stalks baby yu choy (also known
as choy sum)

Fresh cilantro, chopped (optional)

Steamed rice (see page 24), for
serving

PLANT-BASED/PESCATARIAN OPTION
- Bacon or sausage → 1 to 2 plant-based sausages (such as Beyond or Impossible) (sauté for 4 to 5 minutes in step 1)
- Check for seafood products in the kimchi (disregard if pescatarian)
- Fish sauce → GF soy sauce or tamari (disregard if pescatarian)

SUB
If you can't find gochugaru or Kashmiri chili powder, use ¾ tsp mild paprika + ¼ tsp cayenne.

My recipe for this soul-hugging white bean stew came about when I was craving Korean flavors and found a stash of canned cannellini beans lying around in the cupboard. Although the traditional version doesn't use cannellini beans, it's a great economical dish that builds flavor from simple aromatics and staple ingredients in my gluten-free pantry. With a well-stocked pantry, you'll discover the joys of cooking meals without having to go to the store.

1. In a medium saucepan or wok, heat the cooking oil on medium heat until it shimmers. Add the bacon and sauté until the fat has rendered, about 6 to 8 minutes. Drain off all but about 1 tablespoon of fat (see note).

2. Increase the heat to medium-high, add the mushrooms, and sauté for 3 to 4 minutes, until browned. Reduce the heat to medium, add the garlic and onions, and sauté for 3 to 4 minutes, until softened and fragrant. Add the wine to deglaze the pot, scraping up any browned bits, until the liquid has evaporated.

3. Stir in the water, kimchi, beans, brown sugar, miso, chili flakes, fish sauce, and sesame oil. Bring to a boil, then reduce the heat to low and simmer for 7 minutes, stirring occasionally, until the bean starches have released to thicken the stew. Add the yu choy and simmer for 3 minutes, stirring a few times.

4. Ladle into bowls and garnish with cilantro (if using). Serve with steamed rice.

NOTE
Pour the excess fat from the pan into an empty can to dispose of once it has cooled. Place the can in the fridge to speed up the process.

Cannellini beans are sometimes labeled as white kidney beans or Great Northern beans.

TOMATO, EGG & PESTO STIR-FRY

Inspired by home-cooked
meals and my love of pesto
♫ *Simple Step (feat. Antwaun Stanley)
– Vulfpeck*

SERVES 2

In a Chinese household, the pairing of tomato and egg is the best friend you can always count on. It's easygoing, dependable, and comes through when you need it the most. Typically, eggs are quickly scrambled and then enveloped in saucy and savory simmered tomatoes, but my version has a few twists! I've ditched the gluten-filled Shaoxing wine and oyster sauce, and added pesto for extra herbaceousness, 'cause I love a tomato and basil dish.

2 tbsp neutral high-heat cooking oil

4 large eggs

½ tsp kosher salt

2 large heirloom or hothouse tomatoes, cut into large wedges (see note)

1-inch knob ginger, minced

1 scallion, white and green parts separated, chopped

¼ cup water

1 tsp GF fish sauce

1 tsp GF soy sauce or tamari

1 tsp maple syrup

2 tsp cornstarch

2 tsp cool water

1 tbsp Thai Basil Pesto (page 31) or store-bought pesto

Steamed rice (see page 24), for serving

VEGETARIAN OPTION

Fish sauce → additional GF soy sauce or tamari

1. In a large nonstick frying pan or wok, heat 1 tablespoon of the oil on medium-high heat until it shimmers. Meanwhile, in a small bowl, beat the eggs and salt with a fork. Pour into the pan and scramble with a rubber spatula for 1 to 2 minutes, until the eggs are set but still wet. Transfer to a plate and set aside.

2. Add the remaining oil to the pan. Add the tomatoes, ginger, and white scallions and sauté for 1 minute. Add the ¼ cup water, fish sauce, soy sauce, and maple syrup and simmer for 6 to 7 minutes, until the tomatoes are quite saucy but still somewhat intact.

3. In a small bowl, mix the cornstarch with the 2 teaspoons of cool water to make a slurry. Pour into the pan and simmer for 1 minute or until thickened. Return the scrambled eggs to the pan and mix gently to combine.

4. Portion the eggs into shallow bowls, garnish with the green scallions, and dollop with pesto. Serve with steamed rice.

NOTE

If you're using out-of-season tomatoes, add 1 tablespoon of tomato paste to the ¼ cup of water to amp up the flavor.

FISH SAUCE OYAKODON

MAKES ONE 8-INCH OMELET, SERVES 1 TO 2

Inspired by the original Japanese Iron Chefs

♫ *Put Your Records On* – *Corinne Bailey Rae*

I first ate oyakodon in my early teens, and it reminds me of how amazingly diverse Toronto is as a food city, where restaurants offer home-style dishes like this delicious Japanese chicken and egg rice bowl. It uses the power of eggs to create a super-simple and substantial meal, flavored with gluten-free soy sauce and mirin. The prep is bare bones and, for even more simplicity, I've replaced traditional dashi (bonito fish stock) with fish sauce. This recipe makes one omelet, but could stretch to feed two, for those lounge-in-sweats-at-home kind of nights.

¼ cup water

1½ tbsp GF soy sauce or tamari

1½ tbsp mirin, or 1 tbsp unsalted cooking sake + ½ tbsp maple syrup

¼ tsp GF fish sauce

1 tsp neutral high-heat cooking oil

¼ yellow onion, thinly sliced

1 to 2 boneless skinless chicken thighs, cut into 1-inch pieces

2 large eggs, beaten

1 scallion, sliced on a diagonal

Steamed rice (see page 24), for serving

GF furikake (see note) or sesame seeds, to garnish

VEGETARIAN/PESCATARIAN OPTION

- Chicken thighs → 4 oz (115 g) cremini, oyster, or shiitake mushrooms, stems removed and caps sliced

- Fish sauce → additional GF soy sauce or tamari (disregard if pescatarian)

1. In a measuring cup, combine the water, soy sauce, mirin, and fish sauce.

2. In an 8-inch nonstick frying pan, heat the oil on medium-high heat until it shimmers. Add the onions and chicken and sauté until lightly browned, about 1 to 2 minutes. Pour in the soy sauce mixture, reduce the heat to medium-low and simmer until the chicken is no longer pink inside, about 5 to 6 minutes.

3. Pour the eggs into the pan and sprinkle the scallions over top. Cover and cook until the eggs are set, about 4 to 6 minutes. The amount of time will depend on the type of burner you have, so watch closely and jiggle the pan to see if the eggs have fully set.

4. Slide the omelet directly over a bowl of steamed rice and garnish with furikake.

NOTES

Furikake, made from sesame seeds, bonito fish flakes, and seaweed, can sometimes contain gluten, so read the ingredients thoroughly.

BIRTHDAY CRAB

SERVES 4 🦀 🌿

Inspired by Saigon Star
Restaurant in Richmond Hill
♫ *Things I Thought Were Mine*
– Alfie Templeman

This curry crab is fit for a celebratory family meal. It made appearances on birthdays throughout my childhood, complete with plastic gloves and seafood crackers. It's a messy one, but boy, is it good. Once you crack open the shell, uncover the succulent white meat beneath, and dip it into the luscious sauce, you'll understand why this dish brings me and my family so much joy. The best part? It's more approachable than you might think and comes together in about 20 minutes. And just when you think the fun is over, you can toast some GF bread to mop up the sauce.

1 tbsp neutral high-heat cooking oil

6 cloves garlic, minced

2 small shallots, minced (about ¼ cup)

2-inch knob ginger, minced

1 cup vegetable, chicken, seafood stock, or Freezer Bag Stock (page 24)

2 tbsp tomato paste

1 tbsp liquid honey

1 tbsp chili paste (such as sambal oelek or Calabrian)

½ tbsp rice vinegar

1½ tsp curry powder

2 tsp cornstarch

2 tsp cool water

1 large egg, beaten

2 lb (900 g) Dungeness crab, separated into leg and claw pieces

Fresh cilantro, chopped

Steamed rice (see page 24), for serving

GF bread, toasted, for serving (see note on page 132)

1. In a medium saucepan or wok, heat the oil on medium heat until it shimmers. Add the garlic, shallots, and ginger and sauté until aromatic, about 1 to 2 minutes.

2. Stir in the stock, tomato paste, honey, chili paste, rice vinegar, and curry powder, and let it come to a simmer.

3. In a small bowl, mix the cornstarch with the cool water to make a slurry. Pour into the pan and simmer until thickened. (Make a little more slurry if you prefer a thicker sauce.) Stir in the egg and cook for 1 minute.

4. Add the crab and bring to a boil. Reduce the heat to low, cover, and steam for 5 to 7 minutes, until the crab meat is opaque and the shells are bright orange.

5. Portion the crab into bowls, ladle sauce over top, and garnish with cilantro. Serve with steamed rice and GF toast.

NOTES

If you can get live crab in your area, ask the fishmonger to break it down into leg and claw pieces. If live crab is hard to source, feel free to make the same sauce for lobster or shrimp.

Get yourself a seafood cracker or two for easier eating.

STIR-FRIED CHICKEN THIGHS
with Basil

Inspired by three-cup chicken

♫ *Always This Late (Instrumental)* – ODESZA

SERVES 2 TO 4

This recipe is my effortless rendition of Taiwanese three-cup chicken, perfect for a TV dinner kinda night. The name "three-cup chicken" stems from the essential trio of sesame oil, tamari, and cooking wine, all used in equal parts in the original. However, I believe the aromatics play an equally vital part. Alongside smashed garlic and ginger, fresh basil is especially crucial, with its distinctive anise flavor. You know you're Chinese when the first time you ever tasted basil was in the traditional version of this dish!

1 tbsp neutral high-heat cooking oil

2 cloves garlic, smashed

1-inch knob ginger, smashed

1 lb (450 g) boneless skinless chicken thighs, cut into bite-sized pieces

¼ cup unsalted chicken stock, vegetable stock, or Freezer Bag Stock (page 24)

½ tbsp brown sugar or maple syrup

2 tbsp unsalted cooking wine or sake

1½ tbsp GF soy sauce or tamari

¼ tsp freshly cracked white or black pepper

1 tbsp toasted sesame oil

4 sprigs fresh basil (Thai or Italian), leaves torn, or Thai Basil Pesto (page 31)

Steamed rice (see page 24), for serving

1. In a medium nonstick frying pan or wok, heat the cooking oil on medium-high heat until it shimmers. Add the garlic and ginger and sauté until fragrant, about 1 minute. Add the chicken and cook, tossing frequently, until nicely browned but not fully cooked through.

2. Reduce the heat to medium. Stir in the stock, brown sugar, cooking wine, soy sauce, and pepper. Drizzle in the sesame oil and simmer for 6 to 8 minutes, stirring occasionally, until the chicken is no longer pink inside and the sauce has reduced (see note).

3. Turn off the heat and stir in the basil until just wilted (or simply stir in the pesto).

4. Ladle into bowls and serve with steamed rice.

> **NOTE**
> If you prefer a thicker sauce, mix 2 teaspoons cornstarch with 2 teaspoons cool water into a slurry. Pour into the pan at the end of step 2 and simmer until the sauce thickens and clings to the chicken.

FRIED AND SIZZLED

I cook a wide range of things in my nonstick wok, from simple eggs to experimental pasta creations. When I first moved out to go to culinary school, my mom gifted me three kitchen necessities that she can't live without as a non-fussy cook: a rice cooker, a toaster oven, and a nonstick wok. I've learned to use all three religiously (you know from the previous chapter that I'm all about the rice cooker; I'll get to the toaster oven in the next one).

For home cooks, the convenience of cooking in, cleaning, and maintaining a nonstick wok is hard to beat. It's the ideal choice to venture into the world of wok cooking. I've waxed poetic about it on page 8.

In this chapter, you'll discover quick-to-execute recipes stir-fried in a wok or fried in a pan, with replacements for the usual convenient but gluten-filled staples. Fried and crispy dishes are usually off-limits on a gluten-free diet, but, of course, I've made recipes that are equally indulgent, since I know how much of a treat that can be.

Some recipes, such as the Pork & Watercress Crystal Dumplings (page 155) and Salmon Burgers with Sesame Chili Mayo (page 159), require prep ahead of time, but once that's done, they conveniently come together for an easy meal. Mise en place, the practice of having all your ingredients chopped and measured before you start cooking, is essential here to ensure a smooth and enjoyable cooking experience. After making the dishes in this chapter, your nonstick wok will become your number one pan.

Scan me to listen along!

VIETNAMESE-STYLE BREAKFAST SMASH BURGERS

with Fried Eggs

SERVES 4

Inspired by bún chả in Hanoi

♫ *I Try – Macy Gray*

This is essentially my take on a Sausage McMuffin, featuring pork patties from my favorite Northern Vietnamese dish, bún chả, where they're served alongside vermicelli and a tangy fish dipping broth. In this breakfast version, the patties are served on gluten-free brioche buns with a chili onion mayo, pickled veg, fresh cilantro, and a fried egg—the ultimate weekend brunch to revive from a late night.

CHILI MAYO

4 tbsp mayonnaise

2 tsp chili paste (such as sambal oelek or Calabrian), or 1 tsp harissa

½ tsp onion powder

PATTIES

1 lb (450 g) lean or medium ground pork

3 stalks lemongrass, white parts only, finely chopped, or 1 tbsp lemon zest

2 small shallots, minced (about ¼ cup)

2 cloves garlic, minced

1 tbsp maple syrup

1 tbsp GF fish sauce

½ tsp freshly cracked black pepper

½ tsp kosher salt

2 tbsp neutral cooking oil

4 large eggs

4 GF buns (such as Promise or O'doughs) or English muffins (such as Glutino)

Pickled Veg (page 25)

Fresh cilantro, mint, and/or basil (Thai or Italian) leaves

1. **MAKE THE CHILI MAYO:** In a small bowl, mix together the mayonnaise, chili paste, and onion powder.

2. **MAKE THE PATTIES:** Cut four 5-inch squares of parchment paper. In a large bowl, knead together the pork, lemongrass, shallots, garlic, maple syrup, fish sauce, pepper, and salt. Divide the mixture into four balls (4 oz/115 g each). On a cutting board, place a piece of parchment over each meatball and smash with a plastic flipping spatula until the patties are flat.

3. In a large nonstick frying pan, heat 1 tablespoon of the oil on medium heat until it shimmers. Fry the patties for 2 to 3 minutes per side until golden brown on both sides and no longer pink inside.

4. In a medium or another large nonstick frying pan, heat the remaining oil on medium heat until it shimmers. Crack the eggs into the pan and cook either sunny side up (cover and cook for 2½ minutes) or over easy (leave uncovered and cook for 2 minutes, then flip and cook for 30 seconds). Transfer the eggs to a plate lined with a paper towel until ready to serve.

5. Toast the buns and spread the chili mayo over them. Assemble each burger with a patty, fried egg, pickled veg, and herbs.

NOTES

Brioche buns by Promise are our favorite gluten-free burger buns; in these sandwiches, they actually envelop the yolky egg.

Freeze extra patties on individual squares of parchment paper on a baking sheet or platter, then transfer them to a storage bag once they're completely frozen. Store in the freezer for up to 3 months. Reheat frozen patties in a nonstick pan with a drizzle of oil on medium-low-heat for an extra 3 to 4 minutes per side.

'SHROOM TOAST

with Chili Miso

Inspired by foraging for mushrooms
with my brother-in-law
♫ Call Me
- St. Paul & The Broken Bones

MAKES 4 TOASTS, SERVES 2 TO 4

When you want a little indulgence with little effort, reach for this mushroom toast. Charred garlicky mushrooms over lightly toasted bread is hard not to love, especially if you've found some good-lookin' mushrooms at the farmers market. Top it all off with a yolky poached egg, a drizzle of my game-changing Chili Miso Sauce, and Simple Dressed Greens for a luxurious alternative to our friend avo toast.

1 tbsp neutral high-heat cooking oil, plus more as needed

8 oz (225 g) cremini mushrooms, stems removed and caps sliced

8 oz (225 g) shimeji, oyster, shiitake, or chanterelle mushrooms, tough stems removed and caps torn into bite-sized pieces

2 small shallots, minced (about ¼ cup)

2 tsp GF soy sauce or tamari

1 tsp toasted sesame oil

1 tbsp unsalted butter

½ recipe Chili Miso Sauce (page 29)

1 tsp white vinegar

4 large eggs

4 slices GF bread

2 portions Simple Dressed Greens (page 25)

Freshly ground black pepper to taste

DAIRY-FREE/PLANT-BASED OPTION

- Butter → plant-based butter (or omit)
- Plant-based: Omit the poached egg

1. Bring a medium saucepan of water to a boil, then reduce the heat to low to maintain the heat while the mushrooms cook.

2. Meanwhile, in a large nonstick frying pan or wok, heat the cooking oil on medium-high heat until it shimmers. Sauté the mushrooms, tossing frequently, until nicely charred, about 3 to 4 minutes. If the pan gets too dry, add a drizzle of oil.

3. Reduce the heat to medium. Add the shallots and sauté for 1 to 2 minutes, until translucent and fragrant. Reduce the heat to low and add the soy sauce and sesame oil. Add the butter and let it melt. Add a drizzle of chili miso sauce. Turn off the heat and set aside.

4. Line a plate with a few sheets of paper towel. To the pot of hot water, add the vinegar. Increase the heat to medium-low and bring to a simmer. Using a slotted spoon, stir the water to form a gentle whirlpool. Cooking in two batches if needed, crack the eggs, one at a time, into the whirlpool. Poach for 2½ minutes. Gently transfer the eggs to the prepared plate.

5. In a toaster, toast the bread until golden brown.

6. To assemble the toasts, top each piece of toast with mushrooms and a poached egg. Drizzle with chili miso sauce, sprinkle with pepper, and top with the dressed greens.

NOTE

Our top choices for sliced gluten-free bread brands are Promise, Little Northern Bakehouse, Canyon Bakehouse, and Schär.

THE IDEAL STIR-FRY

SERVES 2 🥢 🌱 🍃

Inspired by Mama's quest
for a colorful diet

♫ *Colors – Black Pumas*

When I was growing up, Mama always emphasized that I would get most of my nutrients if I ate the rainbow, so this stir-fry, with its array of vibrant vegetables, is Mama-approved. It's got crisp, fast-cooking veggies, including broccoli, that soak up flavor quickly. Pair it with steamed rice and your choice of protein, like the Roasted Chicken Legs with Pho Broth Gravy (page 197).

1 tbsp neutral high-heat cooking oil

4 oz (115 g) mushrooms (such as cremini, oyster, shiitake, or shimeji), tough stems removed and caps sliced

1 stalk broccoli (about 4 oz/115 g), cut into small florets

½ red, orange, or yellow bell pepper, cut into large squares

½ red onion, cut into large squares

1 cup sugar snap peas, ends and strings removed

2 cloves garlic, minced

½-inch knob ginger, minced

2 tbsp dry white wine or unsalted cooking sake

2 tsp GF soy sauce or tamari

1 tsp chili oil

1 tsp maple syrup

1. In a large nonstick frying pan or wok, heat the cooking oil on medium-high heat until it shimmers. Add the mushrooms and stir-fry, tossing frequently, for 3 minutes or until browned. Add the broccoli, bell peppers, onions, and peas and stir-fry, tossing occasionally, for 2 minutes.

2. Reduce the heat to medium and add the garlic and ginger. Sauté for 1 minute or until fragrant. Add the wine to deglaze, scraping up any browned bits, until the liquid has evaporated. Add the soy sauce, chili oil, and maple syrup, and cook, stirring, for 2 minutes. Serve immediately.

NOTE
If you want this to serve 4 to 6 people, double or triple the quantities of all the ingredients, but stir-fry in batches to ensure a nice char on the vegetables.

FRIED RICE FORMULA

SERVES 2 🔪 🌱 🥕 🌿

Inspired by the prevalence of rice in Asian homes

♫ *Back Pocket – Vulfpeck*

There are a few key elements that make for great fried rice: using dry leftover rice from the fridge, cooking on higher heat for delicious char, and holding off on adding liquid ingredients until the end, to prevent it from getting gloppy. Consider this more of a formula than a recipe, as my fried rice changes depending on what's in my fridge. It all starts with a flavor builder, like earthy mushrooms or sweet Chinese sausage. Then I'll add an easy veg option, like bell peppers or frozen peas or corn, for a pop of brightness and sweetness. Next I'll throw in something punchy, like kimchi or dried shrimp, for extra flave and finish it off with a squeeze of lemon or lime juice for a touch of acidity that ties everything together. Use this formula as a base for consistently delicious fried rice every time, adapting to what's in your fridge.

1 tbsp neutral high-heat cooking oil, plus more for drizzling

4 oz (115 g) mushrooms, or 2 links GF Chinese sausage (lap cheong)

2 cups cooked jasmine or short-grain white rice (see page 24)

2 cloves garlic, minced

1-inch knob ginger, minced

½ yellow onion, diced

1 large egg

½ cup veg (such as chopped bell peppers, frozen peas or corn, or a mix)

4 to 8 oz (115 to 225 g) leftover cooked meat (optional)

¼ cup GF kimchi or dried shrimp (optional)

½ tbsp toasted sesame oil

½ tbsp GF fish sauce

Fresh cilantro, basil (Thai or Italian), scallions, or dill, chopped (optional)

Kosher salt and freshly cracked black pepper to taste

A squeeze of lemon or lime juice

A drizzle of GF chili oil (such as chili crisp) (optional)

1 tbsp roasted sesame seeds or toasted pine nuts (see page 25)

PLANT-BASED/VEGETARIAN OPTION

• Check for seafood products in the kimchi

• Fish sauce → GF soy sauce or tamari

• Plant-based: Omit the egg

1. In a large nonstick frying pan or wok, heat the cooking oil on medium-high heat until it shimmers. Add the mushrooms (the flavor builders) and sauté for 3 minutes. Add the rice and stir-fry for 2 minutes, breaking it up into individual grains as much as possible. Add the garlic, ginger, and onions and sauté for 1 to 2 minutes, until fragrant.

2. Make a crater in the rice and drizzle in a bit of cooking oil. Crack an egg into the crater and scramble with a wooden spoon or rubber spatula until mostly cooked through. Incorporate the egg into the rice.

3. Add the veg and meat (if using) and toss to combine. Add the kimchi (if using), sesame oil, fish sauce, and herbs, tossing to combine. Season with salt and pepper. Finish with a squeeze of lemon juice and a drizzle of chili oil (if using). Serve garnished with sesame seeds.

NOTES

For best results, use leftover rice that's been stored uncovered in the fridge.

For the meat, you can use shredded roasted chicken, chopped cooked steak, chopped grilled pork, or whatever you happen to have on hand.

LAOTIAN-STYLE LETTUCE WRAPS

SERVES 2 TO 4

Inspired by laab

♫ Do It – Tuxedo

Those who know me will describe me as the slowest eater they've ever met, but when these lettuce wraps hit the table, I devour them like Lickitung in that sushi-go-round Pokémon Stadium mini-game. (For anyone who didn't play that formative N64 video game: these wraps disappear quickly.) They're an explosion of acidic and salty flavors, ready in less than 20 minutes—great for solo meals or spontaneous gatherings. You can adjust the lime juice, the chili paste, and (especially) the fish sauce to your liking. The best piece of advice I ever received was to add fish sauce generously, then add a little more.

1 tbsp brown sugar or maple syrup

1½ tbsp GF fish sauce

1½ tbsp lime juice

2 tsp chili paste (such as sambal oelek or Calabrian)

2 tbsp neutral high-heat cooking oil

1 lb (450 g) ground meat (such as pork, beef, chicken, or turkey)

2 cloves garlic, minced

1 small shallot, thinly sliced (about 2 tbsp)

4 to 6 sprigs fresh cilantro, basil (Thai or Italian), and/or mint, chopped

1 bunch Bibb or butter lettuce, torn into individual leaves

Pickled Red Onions (page 25) or Quick Pickled Red Onions (page 25)

PLANT-BASED OPTION

- Ground meat → plant-based ground round (such as Beyond or Impossible)

- Fish sauce → GF soy sauce or tamari (disregard if pescatarian)

1. In a small bowl, whisk together the brown sugar, fish sauce, lime juice, and chili paste until the sugar has dissolved.

2. In a large nonstick frying pan or wok, heat the oil on medium-high heat until it shimmers. Add the ground meat and sauté for 3 to 4 minutes, breaking it up with a wooden spoon, until browned. Add the garlic and shallots and sauté for 1 minute. Stir in the sauce mixture until well combined and cook for 1 to 2 minutes to reduce the sauce a bit. Turn off the heat and stir in the herbs.

3. Transfer to a large serving bowl. Serve on lettuce, with pickled red onions.

NOTES

This recipe easily doubles or triples for larger crowds.

Because of the leaves' rounder shape, tender Bibb or butter lettuce make for the best wraps.

CABBAGE PANCAKES
with Scallions & Yum Yum Sauce

SERVES 2

Inspired by okonomiyaki

♫ *Brazilian Soul (feat. Sofi Tukker), Acoustic Bossa Version – The Knocks*

I first whipped up these savory pancakes during a special plant-based Japanese evening at my intimate pop-up series, Monty's. After several years of working for others in the industry, Monty's was my first solo venture, where I served a rotating tasting menu to over 200 guests. It was a space where I had the freedom to create without boundaries and share my very soul on a plate. These veg-forward pancakes draw inspiration from my family trips to Japan, a place filled with amazing food and great memories. It's a crisp and satiating dish made up of shredded cabbage, carrots, and oyster mushrooms, with this version held together by a rice flour batter and served with guaranteed-gluten-free sauce. Once fried, they're served with savory scallions, gluten-free furikake, and a Japanese-American steakhouse mayo called yum yum sauce that hits just about every taste bud.

YUM YUM SAUCE

¼ cup mayonnaise

2 tbsp ketchup

1 tbsp room-temperature tahini

1 tbsp GF soy sauce or tamari

½ tsp toasted sesame oil

PANCAKES

1 large egg

1 cup room-temperature water

2 tsp GF miso paste

¼ tsp kosher salt

1 cup rice flour

¼ cup GF all-purpose flour

2 cloves garlic, minced

1-inch knob ginger, minced

1 large carrot, julienned

⅛ red cabbage, shredded

⅛ green cabbage, shredded

4 oz (115 g) oyster mushrooms, stems removed and caps torn into pieces

2 tbsp roasted black and/or white sesame seeds

1 tbsp neutral high-heat cooking oil

2 scallions, chopped on a diagonal

GF furikake (optional)

1. **MAKE THE YUM YUM SAUCE:** In a small bowl, mix together the mayonnaise, ketchup, tahini, soy sauce, and sesame oil.

2. **MAKE THE PANCAKES:** In a large bowl, whisk together the egg, water, miso, and salt. Sift in the rice flour and all-purpose flour, mixing to form a batter. Add the garlic, ginger, carrots, red cabbage, green cabbage, mushrooms, and sesame seeds, tossing to combine.

3. In a medium nonstick frying pan, heat the cooking oil on medium heat until it shimmers. Add half of the batter and flatten out into a thin layer with a spatula. Cook for 4 to 6 minutes, until golden brown on the bottom. Cover the pan with a large plate and, in a swift motion, turn the pan upside down to flip the pancake onto the plate. Slide the pancake back into the pan and cook the other side for 4 to 6 minutes, until golden brown. Slide the pancake onto a serving plate. Repeat with the remaining batter.

4. Garnish the pancakes with scallions and drizzle with yum yum sauce and furikake (if using).

FIVE-SPICE DUCK BREAST
with Scallion Crepes

Inspired by Peking duck

♫ *Ms. Ho - Onra*

SERVES 4

I needed to find a way to share the essence of Peking duck with Reid, as the steamed buns and hoisin prevented him from enjoying it with my family at restaurants. This is my at-home, gluten-free rendition! Beautifully browned, five-spiced duck breast is wrapped in simple scallion crepes with homemade hoisin, extra fresh scallions, and crisp cucumbers. It's a showstopper that's straightforward to execute for a fun, family-style meal.

HOISIN

1 tbsp brown sugar or maple syrup

1 tbsp GF soy sauce or tamari

1 tbsp room-temperature tahini

½ tbsp GF miso paste

½ tbsp toasted sesame oil

½ tsp Chinese five-spice powder, or ¼ tsp ground cinnamon + ¼ tsp ground cloves

½ tsp garlic powder

1 tsp water

SCALLION CREPES

1¼ cups GF all-purpose flour

1 tbsp granulated sugar

¼ tsp kosher salt

4 scallions, green parts only, finely chopped

2 large eggs

1½ cups whole milk

A drizzle or spray of neutral high-heat cooking oil

DUCK

2 Muscovy duck breasts (about 1 lb/450 g each)

2 tsp Chinese five-spice, or 1 tsp ground cinnamon + 1 tsp ground cloves

½ tsp kosher salt

½ English cucumber, julienned

8 scallions, julienned, shocked in ice water, and drained

DAIRY-FREE OPTION

Milk → unsweetened non-dairy milk

1. **MAKE THE HOISIN:** In a small bowl, mix together the brown sugar, soy sauce, tahini, miso, sesame oil, five-spice, garlic powder, and water.

2. **MAKE THE SCALLION CREPES:** In a medium bowl, whisk together the flour, sugar, and salt.

3. In a large bowl, whisk together the scallions, eggs, and milk. Add the dry ingredients and mix until uniform in consistency.

4. Lightly drizzle or spray cooking oil in a small nonstick frying pan on medium-low heat. Pour in ¼ cup batter and cook for about 30 seconds, then flip and cook for 30 seconds. Transfer the crepe to a plate. Repeat with the remaining batter.

5. **MAKE THE DUCK:** Using a chef's knife, score the skin side of the duck breasts in a crosshatch pattern. Season both sides of the breasts with five-spice and salt.

6. Heat a cast-iron or nonstick frying pan on medium-high heat. Lay the duck breasts skin side down. Sear for 6 to 8 minutes, until the skin is crispy and golden, lowering the heat if it is browning too quickly. Flip the breasts and cook for 3 to 4 minutes, until they reach an internal temperature of 135°F (57°C) for medium-rare. If you prefer medium, cook for a couple minutes longer to an internal temperature of 145°F (63°C). Transfer to a cutting board, cover with foil, and let rest for 10 minutes to ensure juicy meat. Slice thinly or dice into cubes.

7. Serve the duck on the scallion crepes, with hoisin, cucumber, and scallions.

NOTE
You can keep the duck fat to roast potatoes or cook vegetables. Strain the rendered duck fat through a fine-mesh sieve and store it in an airtight container in the fridge for up to 3 months.

STIR-FRIED RICE NOODLES

with Sausage & Bean Sprouts

Inspired by simple Cantonese chow mein from my childhood

♫ *Busy Earnin' – Jungle*

SERVES 2

You'll be nomming noodles in no time with this simple and satisfying stir-fry that features sausages for convenient flavor, bok choy as a quick-cooking veg, and bean sprouts for something crispy fresh, all seasoned with sweet soy sauce and a sprinkling of ground coriander for a delightful floral note. Fresh rice noodles are always a treat here, but if you're having trouble finding them, wide dried rice sticks work like a charm.

5.3 oz (150 g) dried wide (¼-inch) flat rice noodles

1½ tbsp GF soy sauce or tamari

1 tbsp maple syrup

1 tsp ground coriander

1 tbsp neutral high-heat cooking oil

2 GF honey-garlic sausages, mild Italian sausages, or Mexican chorizo, sliced into bite-sized pieces

2 cloves garlic, minced

¼ yellow onion, thinly sliced

2 heads Shanghai bok choy, ends cut off, chopped into bite-sized pieces

1 tbsp unsalted cooking wine or sake

½ cup bean sprouts

½ tsp toasted sesame oil

1 tbsp roasted sesame seeds

Fresh cilantro, chives, and/or scallion greens, chopped

PLANT-BASED/PESCATARIAN OPTION

Sausage → plant-based sausage (such as Beyond or Impossible)

1. In a large bowl, soak the rice noodles in cool water for at least 30 minutes, until opaque and pliable. Drain in a colander.

2. Meanwhile, in a small bowl, whisk together the soy sauce, maple syrup and coriander.

3. In a large nonstick frying pan or wok, heat the cooking oil on medium heat until it shimmers. Add the sausages and sauté for 2 to 3 minutes, until they are beginning to brown and release fat. Add the garlic and onions and sauté until just fragrant, about 30 seconds.

4. Increase the heat to medium-high. Add the rice noodles and stir-fry for 2 minutes, using tongs or chopsticks to keep the noodles moving. Add the bok choy and stir-fry, tossing frequently, for 1 to 2 minutes, until the greens are just starting to wilt. Add the cooking wine to deglaze, scraping up any browned bits, until the liquid has evaporated. Add the soy sauce mixture and toss to combine, loosening up noodles into individual strands. Turn off the heat and incorporate the bean sprouts.

5. Portion into dishes, drizzle with sesame oil, and garnish with sesame seeds and herbs.

NOTE

Bean sprouts are such a great part of this dish, but I know purchasing a whole bag can feel like a commitment. Store extra bean sprouts in an airtight container filled with cold water in the fridge to prolong their life. If you're looking for another way to use them, add them to scrambled eggs and serve with rice and a bit of tamari for an effortless meal.

If you have fresh rice noodles, skip step 1.

PORK & BASIL STIR-FRY

with Crispy Fried Eggs

SERVES 4 🔥 🌱 🍴 🌿

Inspired by pad kra pao

♫ *Skate – Silk Sonic*

This dish is my twist on pad kra pao, a classic Thai comfort meal traditionally made from ground pork, holy basil, and gluten-filled oyster sauce. I opt for Thai or Italian basil, since holy basil is a rare find in North America, plus gluten-free oyster sauce or, when that's not available, an easy mix of soy sauce, brown sugar, and fish sauce. It wouldn't be complete without a crispy fried egg with a yolk that oozes over. A Thai person would tell you this version is "farang (foreigner) spicy" with just a bit of kick, so if you can handle it, toss in a few more chilies!

4 tbsp neutral high-heat cooking oil

1½ lb (675 g) lean or medium ground pork

4 cloves garlic, minced

1 small shallot, thinly sliced (about 2 tbsp)

2 tbsp GF oyster sauce

1 long red Thai chili, thinly sliced, or 2 tsp chili paste (such as sambal oelek or Calabrian)

6 sprigs fresh basil (Thai or Italian) leaves, torn

4 large eggs

Kosher salt and freshly cracked pepper to taste

Steamed jasmine rice (see page 24), for serving

Fresh cilantro, chopped

¼ cup GF fried shallots (optional)

PLANT-BASED/VEGETARIAN/ PESCATARIAN OPTION

• Ground pork → meatless ground round like Impossible or Beyond

• Oyster sauce → my oyster sauce substitute (below) (disregard if pescatarian)

• Plant-based: Omit the eggs

SUB

If you can't find GF oyster sauce, use 1 tbsp GF soy sauce or tamari + ½ tbsp brown sugar or maple syrup + ½ tbsp GF fish sauce.

1. In a large nonstick frying pan or wok, heat 1 tablespoon of the oil on medium-high heat until it shimmers. Add the pork and sauté for 3 to 4 minutes, breaking it up into small pieces with a wooden spoon, until browned. Add the garlic and shallots and sauté for 30 seconds. Add the oyster sauce and chilies. Turn off the heat and stir in the basil.

2. In a medium or large nonstick frying pan, heat the remaining oil on medium-high heat until it shimmers. Crack the eggs into the pan and season with salt and pepper. Tilt the pan to the side so that the oil pools and use a spoon to pour the oil over the egg whites until they're opaque and the edges are crispy, about 1 minute. Transfer to a plate lined with a paper towel.

3. Plate the pork stir-fry over the steamed rice and top each serving with a crispy fried egg. Garnish with cilantro and fried shallots (if using).

SHANGHAI STIR-FRIED GNOCCHI

Inspired by Shanghai stir-fried rice cakes

♫ *You Make Me Feel Like Dancing - Leo Sayer*

SERVES 3 TO 4 🍶 ♣ 🌿

This dish is a good example of my culinary identity and the type of food I want to share in this book: Asian-inspired gluten-free eats using ingredients that are readily available in North America. It's my riff on Shanghai rice cakes, which often call for oyster sauce containing gluten. Although there are gluten-free rice cakes out there (I use them in recipes like Rice Cake Soup on page 72), they can be hard to find and aren't guaranteed to be gluten-free. Gluten-free gnocchi is easier to track down and makes for a fun take on this dumpling house classic.

1 lb (450 g) GF potato gnocchi

2 tsp brown sugar or maple syrup

2 tsp GF soy sauce or tamari

2 tsp GF fish sauce

2 tbsp neutral high-heat cooking oil, plus more as needed

8 oz (225 g) shiitake mushrooms, stems removed and caps sliced

2 boneless skinless chicken thighs, cut into small strips

2 scallions, white and green parts separated, chopped

½ yellow onion, thinly sliced

1 cup chopped napa cabbage

2 cloves garlic, minced

1-inch knob ginger, minced

½ lemon, for squeezing

A drizzle of toasted sesame oil or GF chili oil (such as chili crisp)

PLANT-BASED/PESCATARIAN OPTION

- Fish sauce → additional GF soy sauce or tamari (disregard if pescatarian)
- Omit the chicken

1. Bring a medium pot of salted water to a boil. Add the gnocchi and cook for 1 minute less than the package instructions (they'll continue to cook when stir-fried). Drain in a colander and run under cold water to prevent the gnocchi from sticking together and to stop them from cooking further.

2. In a small bowl, mix the brown sugar, soy sauce, and fish sauce until well combined.

3. In a large nonstick frying pan or wok, heat 1 tablespoon of the cooking oil on medium-high heat until it shimmers. Add the mushrooms and sauté, tossing frequently, for 2 to 3 minutes, until nicely charred. If the pan becomes dry, drizzle in more oil. If there is too much moisture in the pan, let it evaporate before continuing.

4. Add the chicken and sauté, tossing frequently, for 2 to 3 minutes, until just browned. Add the white scallions, onions, and cabbage and stir-fry for 2 minutes. Add the garlic and ginger and toss until fragrant, about 1 minute. Transfer the stir-fry to a large bowl.

5. Reduce the heat to medium and add the remaining cooking oil. Add the gnocchi and cook for 2 to 3 minutes, until browned and slightly crispy. Return the stir-fry mixture to the pan and stir in the sauce mixture and green scallions.

6. Finish with a squeeze of lemon juice and serve with a drizzle of sesame or chili oil.

NOTE

If you can find GF flat, Chinese, or Korean rice cakes, by all means use them instead of gnocchi. Skip step 1 and stir-fry them directly from the package.

MINCED PORK NOODLES

with Cucumbers

SERVES 4 🔥 🌱 🍃

Inspired by zhajiangmian

♫ *Superstition – Stevie Wonder*

After much experimenting, I've discovered that gluten-free spaghetti reigns supreme as the simplest and most effective substitute for wheat noodles, due to its similar texture. Here, it serves as the base for a saucy Chinese ragu and refreshing julienne cucumbers, my GF version of zhajiangmian—a lick-your-lips type of slurpable noodle dish I've enjoyed at dumpling shops across Toronto.

10½ oz (300 g) dried GF spaghetti

2 tbsp neutral high-heat cooking oil, plus a drizzle

1 lb (450 g) ground pork, chicken, or turkey

4 cloves garlic, minced

2-inch knob ginger, grated

3 tbsp GF fermented black beans, roughly chopped

2 tbsp GF gochujang (Korean chili paste)

1 tbsp GF soy sauce or tamari

1 tbsp toasted sesame oil

¼ tsp Chinese five-spice powder, or a pinch of ground cinnamon + a pinch of ground cloves

2 cups unsalted chicken stock, vegetable stock, or Freezer Bag Stock (page 24)

1½ tbsp cornstarch

1½ tbsp cool water

½ English cucumber, julienned

Fresh cilantro, chopped

PLANT-BASED/PESCATARIAN OPTION

Ground pork → plant-based ground round (such as Beyond or Impossible)

SUBS

• If you can't find GF fermented black beans, substitute chopped kalamata olives.

• If you can't find GF gochujang, substitute 1 tbsp GF miso paste + 1 tbsp chili paste (such as sambal oelek or Calabrian) + 2 tsp maple syrup.

1. Bring a large pot of salted water to a boil. Add the spaghetti and cook according to package instructions, stirring occasionally to ensure the noodles don't clump together. Drain in a colander and drizzle with a bit of cooking oil to prevent sticking.

2. Meanwhile, in a large nonstick frying pan or wok, heat the cooking oil on medium-high heat until it shimmers. Add the pork and sauté for about 3 to 4 minutes, breaking it up with a wooden spoon, until browned. Add the garlic and ginger and sauté for 1 minute. Stir in the black beans, gochujang, soy sauce, sesame oil, and five-spice.

3. Stir in the stock, reduce the heat to medium-low, and simmer for 5 minutes, stirring occasionally.

4. In a small bowl, mix the cornstarch with the cool water to make a slurry. Slowly pour it into the pan and stir until thickened.

5. Use your fingers to loosen up the noodles, then portion them into large bowls. Spoon the ragu over top and garnish with the cucumbers and cilantro.

CHICKEN THIGH KATSU

SERVES 4 🍴

Inspired by Curry House in LA

♫ *Popular Mechanics For Lovers – Beulah*

Gluten-free fam: meet the fried chicken cutlets of your dreams! Non-gluten-free fam: whip up this dish for your gluten-free peeps and watch as you become their culinary hero. In fact, these might just become everyone's fave fried chicken cutlets! Crispy gluten-free foods are actually quite easy to master, since gluten's usual role as a binder isn't needed. Plus, with the relatively wide availability of gluten-free panko, this recipe is a breeze. It's crispy, it's juicy, and the toasted sesame seeds make the crust extra nutty and special. Serve it with Crisp Cabbage Slaw (page 51), or alongside Japanese-Style Curry (page 113) and Steamed Rice (page 24) for a heartier meal.

1½ lb (675 g) boneless skinless chicken thighs (about 6 to 10)

1 tsp kosher salt, plus more to taste

Freshly cracked black pepper

¼ cup rice flour

2 large eggs, beaten

1½ cups GF panko or breadcrumbs

⅓ cup white sesame seeds

1 cup neutral high-heat cooking oil

1. Open the chicken thighs and lay them out on a large cutting board. Season with the salt and several grinds of pepper.

2. Put the rice flour and eggs in separate pie plates or shallow bowls. In a third pie plate or shallow bowl, mix the panko and sesame seeds. Dredge each thigh in rice flour, then in egg, then in the panko mixture, tapping off any excess along the way. Place on a large baking sheet.

3. Line another baking sheet with a few layers of paper towel and place a wire rack on top.

4. In a cast-iron pan or Dutch oven, heat the oil on medium-high heat to 350°F (180°C) until it shimmers. It will be thin and shimmering. Add the chicken in batches and fry for 2 to 3 minutes per side, until crispy golden and the internal temperature reaches 160°F (71°C). Transfer the cooked chicken to the wire rack and let cool for a few minutes, then season with salt.

NOTES

Kikkoman, PaneRiso, and Kinnikinnick gluten-free panko are all good store-bought options. Alternatively, you can make your own gluten-free breadcrumbs: blitz frozen gluten-free bread ends in a blender or food processor.

Let the oil you used to fry the chicken cool completely, then strain it into an airtight container. You can store it for up to 1 month and reuse it to fry other foods.

PORK & WATERCRESS CRYSTAL DUMPLINGS

Inspired by
Mama Lo's dumplings
♫ *Golden – Cory Wong
and Cody Fry*

MAKES 45 TO 50 DUMPLINGS

These dumplings hold a special place in my heart. The filling is my mom's recipe, a favorite when we gathered around the table to bundle a batch as a whole fam. The wrappers are a twist on Chiu-Chow–style fun guo, using a blend of tapioca starch, rice flour, and glutinous rice flour, making them perfect for me to share with Reid. Mastering the dough can take a bit of practice, but once you get the hang of it, these dumplings will become your all-time faves! Enjoy them steamed or pan-fried, best served with my Dumpling Sauce. If you don't have a gluten allergy, use this filling with premade wrappers.

TOOLS

Bench scraper or butter knife

Large ziplock bag

Tortilla press or rolling pin

WRAPPERS

1½ cups water

1¼ cups tapioca starch

¾ cup white rice flour, plus more for dusting

½ cup glutinous rice flour

½ tsp kosher salt

2 tbsp neutral high-heat cooking oil

FILLING

1 lb (450 g) lean or medium ground pork

2 large eggs, beaten

2 tbsp GF soy sauce or tamari

1 tbsp GF oyster sauce

1 tsp toasted sesame oil

4 sprigs fresh cilantro and/or scallions, chopped

4 cloves garlic, minced or grated

2-inch knob ginger, minced or grated

1 large handful of watercress or spinach, thick stems removed, chopped

¼ tsp freshly cracked white or black pepper

1. **MAKE THE WRAPPERS:** In a small saucepan, bring the water to a boil.

2. Meanwhile, in a large bowl, whisk together the tapioca starch, rice flour, glutinous rice flour, salt, and cooking oil until evenly combined.

3. Stabilize the bowl by wrapping a damp rag around the bottom. Slowly pour in a steady stream of boiled water as you use a wooden spoon to mix the dough. Don't pour all of the water in at once; it's much easier to add water later than it is to fix a wet dough! Stop pouring once the dough reaches the consistency of a shaggy, lumpy ball; you might only use 1¼ cups of water.

4. Wait until the dough is cool enough to touch, then knead with your hands, pushing with your knuckles and pulling back with your fingers. Most of the dough will form into clumps, with some drier crumbs along the edges of the bowl. Incorporate these dry crumbs as you knead for 2 solid minutes, until smooth and taut. Add a dusting of rice flour if the dough is sticking to your hands. The dough is a Goldilocks situation: it should be not too dry and not too sticky, similar to the consistency of playdough.

5. Form the dough into a smooth ball, wrap in plastic wrap, and rest on the counter for 30 minutes, with the bowl flipped upside down as a cover.

6. **MEANWHILE, MAKE THE FILLING:** In another large bowl, mix the pork, eggs, soy sauce, oyster sauce, sesame oil, half of the cilantro, garlic, ginger, watercress, and pepper until the ingredients are evenly distributed.

7. **FORM AND FILL THE DUMPLINGS:** Cut two 6-inch squares from the large ziplock bag. Dust the counter with rice flour. Using the bench scraper, divide the dough into 45 to 50 even pieces (about 13 to 15 grams each) and form each into a rough sphere. Cover the spheres with the large bowl to prevent them from drying out while you make the dumplings.

CONTINUED

COOK & SERVE

1 to 2 tbsp neutral high-heat cooking oil (optional, if frying)

Dumpling Sauce (page 29), for serving

VEGETARIAN/PESCATARIAN OPTION

- Ground pork → plant-based ground round (such as Beyond or Impossible)
- Oyster sauce → ½ tbsp GF soy sauce or tamari + ½ tbsp maple syrup (disregard if pescatarian)

SUB

If you can't find GF oyster sauce, use 1½ tsp GF soy sauce or tamari + ¾ tsp brown sugar or maple syrup + ¾ tsp GF fish sauce

NOTES

For pliable dough, it's very important to use freshly boiled water.

For twisted rope folds: Once you've folded a half moon, fold diagonally from the right-hand corner if you're right-handed, or the left-hand corner if you're left-handed. Continue with consecutive diagonal folds, twisting smoothly, until you reach the opposite side.

To freeze steamed dumplings: Transfer the dumplings to a parchment-lined baking sheet drizzled with oil to cool completely. Wrap the entire pan in plastic wrap and freeze for 1 to 3 hours. Transfer the frozen dumplings to ziplock bags and store in the freezer for up to 3 months. Reheat in a steamer for 3 to 4 minutes, or fry in a drizzle of oil on medium-low heat, covered, for about 3 minutes per side.

8. Using the tortilla press, smush one of the spheres between the cut ziplock squares to form a circular wrapper. (If you don't have a tortilla press, use a rolling pin to roll out the sphere between the plastic squares to between 3 and 3½ inches in diameter.) If the dough is sticky, dust with additional flour. The wrappers should be pliable and sturdy, not easily breakable.

9. Delicately peel off the top layer of plastic. Flip the flattened dough onto the dusted counter, with the second sheet of plastic still on, then delicately peel off the plastic. Dust the top with rice flour.

10. Using the bench scraper, pick up the wrapper and add about 2 teaspoons of filling to the center. Fold the wrapper in half and press firmly but delicately along the edges to seal—this is called a half-moon fold. If you're feeling fancy, you can try the fold featured in the photo, called a twisted rope (see note), but the half-moon fold is easiest for this delicate gluten-free dough. Place the dumpling on a parchment-lined baking sheet.

11. Repeat steps 8 to 10 with the remaining dough and filling. You can begin cooking a batch as soon as you have assembled enough to fill a basket, continuing to form and fill while it cooks.

12. **COOK THE DUMPLINGS:** Set up your steamer basket in a Dutch oven (see the sidebar on page 8). Place a few dumplings in the parchment-lined basket, making sure there's plenty of space between them so they don't stick together, and steam for 6 minutes or until the filling is cooked through. Set the cooked dumplings on a plate or platter, and continue to steam the rest in batches. (After steaming, some or all of the dumplings can be frozen; see note.)

13. For crispy dumplings (if desired), in a large nonstick frying pan, heat 1 tablespoon of cooking oil on medium heat until it shimmers. Working in batches, fry the steamed dumplings for about 2 minutes per side, until both sides are golden brown. Add more oil as needed between batches.

14. Serve garnished with the remaining cilantro, with dumpling sauce on the side.

DUMP THE HATE

These dumplings also represent a defining moment in my life. In March 2021, I kickstarted a campaign called Dump the Hate, uniting a global community to make over 45,000 dumplings and raising more than $150,000 for organizations fighting against Asian hate crimes. This movement not only brought people together, but also empowered me to proudly embrace my identity as an Asian woman.

SALMON BURGERS

with Sesame Chili Mayo

Inspired by
my personal cheffing days
♫ *Inside And Out – Feist*

MAKES 8 BURGERS

At one point, I landed an awesome gig as a personal chef for my good friend and his pescatarian fam, and salmon burgers were a huge hit. This Asian-inspired version with ginger and coriander has become a staple whenever Reid and I are in the mood for something light and satisfying. For best results, use a food processor to make the salmon mixture; this works the proteins in the egg whites and helps bind the patties together. Once cooked, top the patties off with my favorite fixings: lettuce, juicy tomatoes, tender herbs (of course), and a craveable Sesame Chili Mayo that comes together in a snap.

2 lb (900 g) skinless salmon fillets, cut into 1-inch cubes (see note)

4 small shallots, sliced (about ½ cup)

4 cloves garlic, sliced

2-inch knob ginger, sliced

2 large egg whites

2 tbsp maple syrup, or 1½ tbsp liquid honey

2 tbsp GF soy sauce or tamari

1 tsp ground coriander

½ cup GF panko or breadcrumbs

1 tsp kosher salt

1 to 2 tbsp neutral high-heat cooking oil

8 GF buns (such as Promise or O'Doughs)

Sesame Chili Mayo (page 30)

8 Bibb or butter lettuce leaves

2 hothouse or heirloom tomatoes, cut into 16 slices

4 sprigs fresh cilantro, dill, and/or basil (Thai or Italian) leaves

1. Place the salmon in the freezer for 20 minutes, until partially frozen. This will help keep the salmon in small bits when cut, rather than turning into a paste. Line a baking sheet with parchment paper and set aside a second piece of parchment paper the same size.

2. In a food processor, blitz the shallots, garlic, and ginger until finely chopped. Don't blend until smooth. Add the salmon, egg whites, maple syrup, soy sauce, and coriander and pulse until uniform but still chunky. If it isn't coming together, pour half into a bowl, blitz the remainder, and transfer to a second bowl. Blitz the remaining half and combine with the rest in a bowl. Add the panko and salt and mix until just combined.

3. Measure ½-cup portions of the salmon mixture and form into patties and place them on the prepared pan. (You can freeze some or all of the patties; see note.)

4. In a large nonstick frying pan, heat 1 tablespoon of oil on medium heat until it shimmers. Working in batches as needed, fry the patties for 2 to 3 minutes per side, until cooked through and golden on both sides, then set aside to rest for 2 minutes off the heat. Add a drizzle of oil between batches if needed.

5. Toast the buns and spread sesame chili mayo over them. Assemble each burger with a patty, lettuce, tomatoes, and herbs.

NOTES

When you're cubing the salmon, if there are any bones remaining in the fillets, remove them with a pair of tweezers.

You can freeze the patties on small baking sheets lined with parchment paper. Once frozen, transfer the patties to a freezer bag and store for up to 3 months. To fry from frozen, fry on medium-low heat for an additional 2 to 3 minutes per side.

COCONUT LIME SHRIMP PASTA

with Parm

SERVES 2 🦐 🌿

Inspired by easy pasta meals

♫ *Dominoes – Jungle*

I used to have hang-ups about pairing cheese with Asian flavors, but then I grew to love dishes like Korean cheesy corn and ramen with mozzarella. Here, umami-rich Parmesan amps up the flave in my take on a rosé sauce while lavishly coating the noodles. It's an unexpected fusion of tastes that harmoniously combines into a beautiful dish. This pasta has turned into a lunchtime staple whenever we have frozen shrimp and spinach in the fridge.

5.3 oz (150 g) dried GF spaghetti or linguine

A drizzle of extra virgin olive oil

1 tbsp unsalted butter

12 oz (340 g) large or jumbo shrimp, peeled and deveined (see note on page 83)

2 cloves garlic, minced

1-inch knob ginger, minced

1 cup full-fat coconut milk

2 tbsp tomato paste

1 tbsp GF fish sauce, soy sauce, or tamari

1 tbsp maple syrup or liquid honey

½ tsp Kashmiri chili powder

2 makrut lime leaves, crumbled (see note)

2 cups (2 oz/60 g) fresh baby spinach

1 cup fresh or frozen corn kernels (about 1 cob)

Zest and juice of ½ lime

Grated Parmesan cheese, to garnish

Fresh cilantro, scallions, or dill, chopped (optional)

DAIRY-FREE OPTION

- Butter → plant-based butter or neutral high-heat cooking oil
- Parmesan → nutritional yeast

SUB

If you can't find Kashmiri chili powder, use ½ tsp mild paprika + ⅛ tsp cayenne.

1. While you're doing your prep, bring a large pot of salted water to a boil. Add the spaghetti and cook for 2 minutes less than the package instructions (it will finish cooking in the sauce). Drain in a colander and drizzle with olive oil to prevent sticking.

2. In a large nonstick frying pan or wok, melt the butter on medium-high heat. Add the shrimp and fry for 1½ minutes per side. Add the garlic and ginger and sauté until fragrant, about 30 seconds.

3. Stir in the coconut milk, tomato paste, fish sauce, maple syrup, chili powder, and lime leaves, reduce the heat to low, and simmer for 2 minutes. Add the spaghetti and gently swirl it around to coat with the sauce. Add the spinach and corn and simmer for 1 to 2 minutes, until the spinach is just wilted and the corn has warmed through. Turn off the heat and stir in the lime zest and juice.

4. Using tongs, twirl the pasta into a ladle to create nice mounds, portioning it out into serving bowls. Ladle the sauce over top and garnish with Parmesan and cilantro (if using).

NOTES

Our favorite gluten-free noodles are Jovial's brown rice spaghetti and Garofalo's spaghetti or linguine, as they hold together better than most.

If you can't find lime leaves, stir in an additional 1 tsp lime zest at the end of step 3.

FRIZZLED SARDINE RICE
with Fried Crispy Eggs

Inspired by Filipino garlic rice and Reid's love of sardines

♫ *Hanoï Café – Bleu Toucan*

SERVES 2 🐀 🌿

This recipe highlights our love of sardines, a food that totally gets a bad rap. Here's why sardines are great: they're packed with protein and omega-3s; they're a budget-friendly pantry item; and they're sustainable, since they're low on the food chain. We keep a constant rotation of sardines on hand for quick, easy, and reliably gluten-free meals. In this recipe, Brisling sardines are frizzled in nuoc cham, a sweet and tangy Vietnamese staple, then served over garlicky rice alongside a yolky fried egg for the ultimate value meal.

4 tbsp neutral high-heat cooking oil

2 cups cooked jasmine rice (see page 24)

2 cloves garlic, minced

Kosher salt and freshly cracked black pepper to taste

1 can (3.75 oz/106 g) Brisling sardines in olive oil (about 16 to 22 sardines), drained with ½ tbsp oil reserved

1 tsp maple syrup, or ¾ tsp liquid honey

½ tsp GF fish sauce

½ tsp lime juice

2 large eggs

Fresh cilantro, scallions, dill, and/or basil (Thai or Italian), chopped

½ lime, for squeezing

GF fried garlic (optional)

1. In a large nonstick frying pan or wok, heat 1 tablespoon of the cooking oil on medium-high heat until it shimmers. Add the rice and stir-fry for 2 minutes, breaking it up into individual grains as much as possible. Add the garlic and sauté for 1 to 2 minutes, until fragrant. Season with salt. Transfer the garlic rice to serving bowls.

2. In the same pan, heat the oil from the sardine can on medium heat until it shimmers. Add the sardines, maple syrup, fish sauce, and lime juice and sauté for 1 to 2 minutes, breaking up the sardines into bite-sized pieces with a wooden spoon, until heated through. Top the rice with sardines.

3. Pour out any excess liquid from the pan. Heat the remaining cooking oil on medium-high heat until it shimmers. Crack the eggs into the pan and season with salt and pepper. Tilt the pan to the side so that the oil pools and use a spoon to pour the oil over the egg whites until they're opaque and the edges are crispy, about 1 minute. Transfer to a plate lined with a paper towel.

4. Top each serving with a fried egg. Garnish with herbs, a squeeze of lime, and (if using) fried garlic.

NOTE
Go for Brisling sardines whenever possible. Since they're smaller, there's no need to pick out any scales or bones, plus they're more delicate in texture and flavor.

FAJITAS WITH CHILI CRISP SOUR CREAM

Inspired by childhood dreams

♫ *September*
– Earth, Wind & Fire

SERVES 4

This is the meal of my childhood dreams. Growing up, I longed for those Old El Paso taco nights I saw on TV: glistening tomato chunks, crisp iceberg lettuce, and chunky ground meat tumbling out of those crunchy shells. Fast-forward 20 years, and this is my own version, packed with flavors that make me dance in my seat—five-spiced flank steak, perfectly seasoned crisp veggies, and chili crisp sour cream, all wrapped in warm corn tortillas.

½ cup sour cream

2 tsp chili crisp

1 tbsp neutral high-heat cooking oil

1 red bell pepper, sliced into strips

1 yellow bell pepper, sliced into strips

1 yellow onion, sliced

Easygoing Flank Steak (page 193), but double the marinade and reserve half

12 corn or GF flour tortillas, warmed in a pan (see note)

Fresh cilantro, chopped

½ lime, cut into wedges

Chili paste (such as sambal oelek or Calabrian) or hot sauce to taste

1. In a small bowl, mix the sour cream and chili crisp.

2. In a large nonstick frying pan or wok, heat the oil on medium-high heat until it shimmers. Add the red peppers, yellow peppers, and onions and sauté, tossing frequently, for 3 to 4 minutes, until just starting to soften. Add the reserved steak marinade and simmer for 3 to 4 minutes, stirring occasionally, until the marinade has reduced and thickened.

3. Lay out the warmed tortillas on plates. Smear a small spoonful of chili crisp sour cream on each tortilla. Top with sliced steak, sautéed vegetables, cilantro, a squeeze of lime, and chili paste.

NOTE
Warm the tortillas by heating them directly in a pan on medium heat, flipping occasionally, or by wrapping them in paper towel and microwaving until warm.

GRILLED AND ROASTED

Tell me you're Asian without telling me you're Asian: your parents never turn on their oven because it's used as pot and pan storage. Full-sized ovens are uncommon in homes across Asia due to limited space, so when my mom and dad moved to Canada, they never felt the need to use their supersized North American oven for its intended purpose. What they do have is a cute little toaster oven that proves to be just as versatile. It's perfect for heating up items that can't fit in a slice toaster and roasting dinners for up to four people.

Ever since I moved out of my parents' place, I've learned to love my North American mega oven. Baking and roasting became routine, and when I met Reid—whose family lives and breathes gas BBQs—I was introduced to the world of grilling. This chapter embodies our collective identity, combining Asian flavor profiles with North American techniques.

At Reid's family cottage, a perfect example of this fusion unfolded. With both sides of our families gathered, my uncle returned from the lake with freshly caught pickerel. While a fish fry was in order, he insisted on steaming the fish. His wish was my command, and I rigged a steaming apparatus on a gas grill using a turkey roaster and a wire rack. Half of us savored steamed fish, while the other half indulged in fried fish and chips. The Steamed Fish en Papillote (page 198) is inspired by this experience—it's a streamlined version of the dish, ideal for those without a big enough steamer setup.

These recipes feature substantial cuts of protein and mouthwatering sides roasted or grilled, all paired with vibrant and punchy seasonings. They're a true celebration of my hyphenated identity, dishes that resonate with both heartwarming nostalgia and exciting exploration.

Scan me to
listen along!

ROASTED WINTER SQUASH

with Nuoc Cham

Inspired by cozy weather

♫ *Constellating*
– James & Evander

SERVES 4

Come fall and winter, we eat an abundance of squash, since it's what we've got, fresh-produce-wise, in the great white north. I love pairing caramelized, roasty squash with punchy nuoc cham and freshly chopped cilantro. It makes for a delightful side to accompany just about any cold-weather meal.

2 lb (900 g) winter squash with delicate edible skin (such as honeynut, acorn, or delicata), halved lengthwise, seeded, and cut into ½-inch-thick slices

2 tbsp neutral high-heat cooking oil

½ tsp kosher salt, plus more to taste

Nuoc Cham (page 29)

A drizzle of good-quality extra virgin olive oil

Freshly cracked black pepper to taste

Fresh cilantro, chopped

2 tbsp GF fried garlic and/or shallots (optional)

½ long red Thai chili, thinly sliced (optional)

PLANT-BASED OPTION

Use GF soy sauce or tamari in the nuoc cham

1. Preheat the oven to 425°F (220°C). Line a baking sheet with parchment paper.

2. In a large bowl, toss the squash with the cooking oil and salt. Transfer to the prepared pan, making sure there's space between each slice. Roast for 20 to 25 minutes, tossing halfway through, until golden and tender.

3. Transfer the roasted squash to a platter and dress with a few spoonfuls of nuoc cham. Drizzle with olive oil and season with salt and pepper. Garnish with cilantro and, if using, the fried garlic and chilies.

CARAMELIZED CHILI MAPLE CARROTS
with Thai Basil Pesto

Inspired by sweater weather

♫ *Before I Let Go – Beyoncé*

SERVES 4

2 lb (900 g) carrots, cut on a diagonal into ½-inch-thick slices

2 tbsp neutral high-heat cooking oil

1 tbsp maple syrup

2 tsp chili paste (such as sambal oelek or Calabrian)

½ tsp kosher salt

Thai Basil Pesto (page 31)

I'm anything but a picky eater, but when it comes to carrots, I can be a bit selective. Specifically, half-cooked carrots just don't do it for me. Follow this recipe and you'll achieve roasted carrots with an amazing tenderness. They're a little spicy, a little glazey, and to take the dish to the next level, I pair them with my peanutty Thai Basil Pesto. As they cool, you'll find it difficult to resist snacking on a few before they make it to the table.

1. Preheat the oven to 400°F (200°C). Line a baking sheet with parchment paper.

2. In a bowl, toss the carrots with the oil, maple syrup, chili paste, and salt. Spread out in a single layer on the prepared pan. Roast for 35 to 40 minutes, flipping after 20 minutes, until caramelized. Serve with pesto.

NOTE
Double the recipe and add the extras to the Roasted Veg Quinoa Bowls (page 55) for lunch the next day.

SICHUAN-STYLE CHARRED BROCCOLI

Inspired by Sichuan-style green beans

♫ *Esperar Pra Ver*
– Poolside and Fatnotronic

SERVES 4 TO 6

This recipe combines my love of broccoli with the punchy flavors of Sichuan-style green beans, a beloved classic in my family. The idea here is to char the broccoli until crisp-tender before tossing it in a blend of garlic, ginger, chili paste, and the intense umami of black bean paste (also known as fermented black soybean paste, and sadly, sometimes containing gluten).

1 lb (450 g) broccoli, cut into large florets

2 tbsp neutral high-heat cooking oil

¼ tsp kosher salt, plus more to taste

2 cloves garlic, minced

1-inch knob ginger, minced

3 tbsp GF black bean paste

1 tbsp chili paste (such as sambal oelek or Calabrian)

1 tbsp water

Freshly cracked black pepper to taste

Fresh cilantro, chopped

Roasted sesame seeds

SUB

If you can't find GF black bean paste, use 1 tbsp GF miso paste + 1 tbsp GF soy sauce or tamari + 1 tbsp chopped kalamata olives or GF fermented black beans

1. Preheat the oven or grill to 400°F (200°C). If using the oven, line a baking sheet with parchment paper. If using a grill, make sure it's clean, then lightly brush the grid with oil.

2. In a large bowl, toss the broccoli with 1 tablespoon of the oil and the salt. Spread out in a single layer on the prepared pan or place directly on the grill. Roast or grill for about 15 minutes, flipping the broccoli a few times with tongs, until nicely charred but still crisp-tender.

3. Meanwhile, in a small saucepan, heat the remaining oil on medium heat until it shimmers. Add the garlic, ginger, black bean paste, and chili paste and cook, stirring, until fragrant and uniform, about 2 minutes. Stir in the water.

4. Return the broccoli to the large bowl, add half of the paste, and season with salt and pepper. Garnish with cilantro and sesame seeds. Transfer the remaining paste to an airtight container, let cool, and store in the fridge for up to 5 days to flavor other vegetables.

NOTE

I swapped out traditional green beans for broccoli in this recipe, but I do love both. If you'd like to use green beans, keep the quantities of all the other ingredients the same, but broil the beans on a parchment-lined baking sheet on high for 5 minutes before tossing them in the aromatic paste.

GRILLED VEG WITH GOMAE

SERVES 4 🔥 🌱 🍃

Inspired by spinach gomae

♫ *South of the River*
– Tom Misch

Come grilling season, I can eat plate after plate of grilled veg—especially this dish. Bell peppers, zucchini, and red onions are quickly charred over high heat, then drizzled with gomae, a Japanese ground sesame dressing that's nutty and tangy in all the right ways. Finish with cilantro (if you love it like I do), and you've got a summer staple by your side.

GOMAE

3 tbsp roasted white sesame seeds

1½ tbsp GF soy sauce or tamari

2 tsp mirin, or 1 tsp unsalted cooking sake + 1 tsp maple syrup

1 tsp rice vinegar

GRILLED VEG

½ red onion, cut into 1-inch-thick rounds

1 yellow bell pepper, halved and cored

1 red bell pepper, halved and cored

1 large zucchini, ends cut off, halved lengthwise

A drizzle of neutral high-heat cooking oil, plus more for brushing the grill

¼ tsp garlic powder

Kosher salt and freshly cracked black pepper to taste

Fresh cilantro, chopped (optional)

1. **MAKE THE GOMAE:** In a mortar and pestle, small blender, or spice grinder, pulverize the sesame seeds into a fine powder. Transfer to a small bowl and mix with the soy sauce, mirin, and rice vinegar.

2. **MAKE THE GRILLED VEG:** Preheat the grill to high heat (500°F/260°C). Make sure the grill is clean, then lightly brush the grid with oil.

3. In a large bowl, toss the onions, yellow peppers, red peppers, and zucchini with the oil, garlic powder, salt, and pepper.

4. Grill the red onions for 6 minutes, flipping halfway through. Wrap them in foil and leave on the grill to keep warm. Grill the remaining vegetables for about 2 minutes per side, until just cooked and nicely charred.

5. Arrange the vegetables on a platter and garnish with herbs (if using). Serve with the gomae dressing.

NOTE
Feel free to switch up the gomae with Thai Basil Pesto (page 31).

ROASTED CAULIFLOWER

with Spicy Miso Tahini & Garlicky Panko

Inspired by Middle Eastern
roasted cauliflower

♫ *Can't Buy the Mood
(Two Another Remix) – Tora*

SERVES 2 TO 4

When you return from the farmers market with a gorgeous cauliflower head and a rumbly tummy, this is the dish to make. After enjoying a few roasted cauli dishes at Middle Eastern restaurants where it was the star of the show, I crafted this version with a nutty, spicy miso tahini. Plus, gluten-free peeps can enjoy the satisfaction of crunchy, garlicky panko as a delightful topping. This dish is especially fun with purple, green, or orange cauliflower.

CAULIFLOWER

1 head cauliflower (about
  2 lb/900 g), sliced into 1-inch-
  thick cross-sections

2 tbsp neutral high-heat cooking oil

¼ tsp kosher salt

GARLICKY PANKO

3 tbsp neutral high-heat cooking oil

1 clove garlic, minced

¾ cup GF panko

⅛ tsp kosher salt

Miso Tahini Dressing (page 28)

Fresh cilantro or parsley, chopped

1. **MAKE THE CAULIFLOWER:** Preheat the oven to 450°F (230°C). Line a baking sheet with parchment paper.

2. Arrange the cauliflower in a single layer on the prepared pan, drizzle with the oil, and season with the salt. Roast for 25 to 30 minutes, turning halfway through, until nicely golden and crisp-tender.

3. **MEANWHILE, MAKE THE GARLICKY PANKO:** In a small frying pan, heat the oil on medium heat until it shimmers. Add the garlic and sauté for a few seconds. Add the panko and salt. Reduce the heat to low and toast until the panko mixture is crispy and golden. Set aside to cool.

4. Using a spatula, transfer the roasted cauliflower to a serving plate. Drizzle miso tahini dressing over top. Garnish with garlicky panko and herbs.

NOTE

Choose the densest cauliflower at the store to ensure the slices stay intact after roasting.

GRILLED CORN
with Kimchi Shrimp Mayo

Inspired by
the restaurant Lasita in LA

♫ *Tadow – Masego and FKJ*

SERVES 4 🦐 🌿

This recipe is a good example of my cooking style—combining simple techniques with bold flavors. While grilled corn is great on its own, I like to elevate it with this kimchi shrimp mayo when I want a special treat. It's high impact with low effort, a total win-win.

4 cobs of corn, in the husk

2 tbsp mayonnaise

2 tbsp GF kimchi, minced

½ tbsp shrimp paste

Fresh cilantro and/or scallions, chopped

1. Preheat a cleaned grill to medium-high heat (400°F/200°C).

2. For each cob of corn, peel off a few layers of husk and use shears to trim off the silk tassels.

3. Place the corn in their husks directly on the grill, cover, and cook for 15 to 20 minutes, turning every 5 minutes, until the husks are nicely charred. Peel off the husks with a kitchen towel and grill the corn for another few minutes, turning frequently to get char marks on all sides, until lightly charred.

4. In a small bowl, combine the mayonnaise, kimchi, and shrimp paste.

5. Serve the charred corn with the kimchi shrimp mayo on the side or drizzled over the corn. Garnish with cilantro.

MISO COD

with Oyster Mushrooms & Bok Choy

SERVES 2 🐟 🌿

Inspired by fam trips to Japan

♫ Sh'qweyla – Schwey

I have fond memories of the food and smells of Japan. Since there is a large age gap between me and my sisters, summer trips there with my parents gave us precious time together while I was in high school. I have yet to go back with Reid, since a lot of the cuisine contains ingredients made with micro-glutens. (Hit me up if you want to help translate and travel to Japan with us!) Throughout the years, we've developed a collection of gluten-free Japanese recipes that we enjoy making at home, like this delicately light miso cod.

3 tbsp GF miso paste (white, yellow, or red)

2 tbsp GF mirin, or 1 tbsp unsalted cooking sake + 1 tbsp maple syrup

1½ tsp GF soy sauce or tamari

12 oz (340 g) boneless skinless cod loin, cut into 2 pieces

1 cup boiling-hot water

1 tbsp neutral high-heat cooking oil

4 oz (115 g) oyster mushrooms, stems removed and caps sliced

1 clove garlic, minced

1 scallion white and green parts separated, chopped

8 oz (225 g) baby or Shanghai bok choy, ends trimmed

Kosher salt to taste

GF furikake, to garnish

Steamed rice (see page 24), for serving

1. In a bowl, whisk together 2 tablespoons of the miso with the mirin and soy sauce. Place the cod in a shallow dish, rub the miso mixture over the cod, cover, and marinate in the fridge for at least 30 minutes or up to overnight.

2. In a small bowl, dissolve the remaining miso in the hot water. Set aside.

3. Preheat the broiler to high, with a rack set in the highest position. Line a baking sheet with foil.

4. Transfer the cod loins to the prepared pan and broil on the top rack for 10 to 14 minutes, until charred, moist, and flaky.

5. Meanwhile, in a wok or medium saucepan, heat the oil on medium-high heat until it shimmers. Add the mushrooms and sauté until lightly charred and just cooked through, about 3 to 4 minutes. Add the garlic and white scallions and sauté for 1 minute.

6. Reduce the heat to medium and add the bok choy, tossing a few times in the mushroom and garlic juice. Stir in the miso mixture and bring to a boil. Reduce the heat to medium-low, cover, and simmer for 2 minutes, until the bok choy has just wilted.

7. Portion the cod, mushrooms, and bok choy into pasta bowls and ladle the miso broth over the fish. Season with salt and garnish with furikake and green scallions. Serve with steamed rice.

CHILI MISO SALMON

SERVES 4 TO 6 🥄 🌿

Inspired by
Mama's roasted salmon steaks

♫ *Samba – Cléa Vincent*

I've lost track of how many times I've made this dish—it's just so reliable. With a chili miso sauce that makes anything it touches delicious (it's also a key part of the 'Shroom Toast with Chili Miso on page 132), and a low-temp roast, this salmon comes out flavorful and moist every time. It works as a quick weeknight meal or as a hassle-free option when having people over. To double the recipe, get a whole side of salmon and serve it family-style.

2 lb (900 g) piece skinless salmon side or fillet

Chili Miso Sauce (page 29)

2 scallions, green parts only, thinly sliced on a diagonal

Steamed rice (see page 24), for serving

1. Preheat the oven to 250°F (120°C). Line a baking sheet with parchment paper.

2. Place the salmon on the prepared pan and glaze with chili miso sauce, fully covering the top and sides. Roast for 20 to 30 minutes, depending on the thickness (20 minutes for a 1-inch-thick piece; 30 minutes for a 2-inch-thick piece). This is a slow and gentle cook, resulting in very moist salmon, so check for doneness frequently. The salmon is done when there is still a slight gradient of pink to light-orange meat in the center.

3. Transfer the fish to a serving platter and garnish with scallions. Serve with steamed rice.

NOTE
Any remaining Chili Miso Sauce can be used for 'Shroom Toast (page 132) or for cooked proteins or vegetables.

CARAMELIZED SWEET CHILI SHRIMP

SERVES 2

Inspired by my mother-in-law

♫ *Congo Bongo – Engelwood*

As much as my culinary roots have shaped how Reid and I eat, he and his family have also influenced my cooking in many ways. They're passionate about grilling, and this platter of succulent shrimp has become a cherished tradition on Christmas Day. The marinade is sweet and tangy, with just a whisper of spice, caramelizing once the shrimp hit the grill. For a shortcut version, use bottled sweet chili sauce and add a good squeeze of lime!

2 cloves garlic, sliced

1 long red Thai chili, sliced

¼ cup granulated sugar

1 tsp kosher salt

6 tbsp water

2 tbsp rice vinegar

1 tbsp cornstarch

1 tbsp cool water

½-inch knob ginger, minced

Neutral high-heat cooling oil, for brushing the grill

1 lb large or jumbo shrimp, peeled and deveined (see note on page 83)

½ lime, for squeezing

1. Preheat a cleaned grill to high heat (500°F/260°C). Lightly brush the grid with oil.

2. Using an immersion blender in a tall cup or a small stand blender, blend the garlic, chili, sugar, salt, water, and rice vinegar until uniform in consistency.

3. In a small saucepan, bring the sauce mixture to a simmer on medium heat. Reduce the heat to low and simmer for 3 minutes, stirring occasionally.

4. Meanwhile, in a small bowl, mix the cornstarch with the cool water to make a slurry. Pour into the pan and stir until the sauce thickens, about 1 minute. Stir in the ginger.

5. Place the shrimp in a large bowl and pour about three-quarters of the sweet chili sauce over top. Give it a large squeeze of lime juice.

6. Grill the shrimp for about 2 minutes per side or until firm, pink, and charred. Baste with more sweet chili sauce to taste, and use any remaining sauce as a dip for the shrimp.

CHA SIU CHICKEN SANDOS

with Sesame Chili Mayo

Inspired by Chinese BBQ pork and MOS Burger

♫ *Foreign Language (feat. Jess) – Flight Facilities*

SERVES 4

While I'm not always the biggest fan of sandwiches (there are too many sad sandwiches out there), these cha siu chicken sandos are one of my faves. This recipe combines the seasonings of Chinese BBQ pork with the teriyaki chicken burger from Japan's MOS Burger for the ultimate crowd pleaser. Marinated chicken thighs are grilled and served on a GF bun with shredded lettuce, bright pickles, and mouthwatering Sesame Chili Mayo. A total treat during grilling season.

1 tsp ginger powder

½ tsp garlic powder

½ tsp Chinese five-spice powder, or ¼ tsp ground cinnamon + ¼ tsp ground cloves

½ tsp mild paprika

2 tbsp brown sugar or maple syrup

2 tbsp GF soy sauce or tamari

1 tsp rice vinegar

6 to 8 boneless skinless chicken thighs (about 1½ lb/675 g)

Neutral high-heat cooling oil, for brushing the grill

4 GF brioche buns (such as Promise or O'doughs)

Sesame Chili Mayo (page 30)

Pickled Veg (page 25)

Fresh cilantro leaves

1. In a large bowl, combine the ginger powder, garlic powder, five-spice, paprika, brown sugar, soy sauce, and rice vinegar. Add the chicken and toss to coat. Cover and marinate in the fridge for at least 30 minutes or up to overnight.

2. Preheat the grill to medium-high heat (400°F/200°C). Make sure the grill is clean, then lightly brush the grid with oil.

3. Grill the chicken for about 4 minutes per side or until the internal temperature reaches 160°F (71°C). Transfer the chicken to a cutting board, cover with foil, and let rest for at least 5 minutes to kill off bacteria.

4. Toast the buns until light golden. Spread sesame chili mayo on each bun. Depending on the size of the chicken thighs, you may have to cut a few in half to fit in the buns, but you'll be serving 1½ to 2 thighs per bun. Assemble each sando with chicken, pickled veg, and cilantro.

> **NOTE**
> For a delicious variation, if you have leftover Scallion Ginger Oil (page 30), mix about 1 tablespoon of it with ½ cup of mayonnaise and use that instead of the Sesame Chili Mayo.

GOCHUJANG CHICKEN WINGS

Inspired by Bonchon

♫ *Palco – Gilberto Gil*

SERVES 2 🍴

These are my ideal chicken wings: lightly sauced, with a crisp exterior. The recipe comes together quickly, since the wings are simply grilled or roasted until crispy and golden, then tossed in a punchy gluten-free gochujang sauce. Make it a celebratory summer meal with Grilled Corn with Kimchi Shrimp Mayo (page 178) and Tomatoes with Feta & Scallion Ginger Oil (page 35).

2 lb (900 g) chicken wings, separated into drumettes and flats

1 tbsp neutral high-heat cooking oil, plus more for brushing the grill or rack

1 tsp kosher salt

GOCHUJANG SAUCE

2 tbsp GF gochujang (Korean chili paste)

2 tbsp maple syrup

2 tbsp rice vinegar

1 tbsp GF miso paste

1 tsp toasted sesame oil

A few scallions, chopped (optional)

1 tbsp roasted sesame seeds

SUB

If you can't find GF gochujang, use 1 tbsp GF miso paste + 1 tbsp chili paste (such as sambal oelek or Calabrian) + 1 tsp maple syrup.

1. Preheat the grill or oven to 400°F (200°C). If using the grill, make sure it's clean, then lightly brush the top rack with cooking oil. If using the oven, line a baking sheet with foil, place a wire rack on top, and brush the rack with oil.

2. In a large bowl, toss the chicken wings with the cooking oil and salt until evenly coated.

3. Place the wings on the top rack of the grill or on the rack on the prepared pan. Grill or roast for 15 to 20 minutes, until golden and the internal temperature reaches 160°F (71°C).

4. Meanwhile, in a large bowl, combine the gochujang, maple syrup, rice vinegar, miso, and sesame oil.

5. Increase the grill temperature to high (500°F/260°C) or switch the oven to a high broil. If grilling, lightly brush the main grid with oil and transfer the wings to that grid. Char the wings for 3 to 5 minutes per side, until crispy and golden brown. (Flip frequently if they're on the grill; just once if they're under the broiler.)

6. In a large bowl, toss the wings with the gochujang sauce. Garnish with scallions (if using) and sesame seeds.

SESAME TUNA STEAKS

with Ponzu

Inspired by my internship at
Deville Dinerbar in Montreal

♫ *Coming Alive – Two Another*

SERVES 2

When fresh, good-lookin' sustainable tuna is available at the store, this recipe is a no-brainer. Ahi tuna is a special treat kind of protein, versatile enough to elevate salads (Tuna & Curry-Roasted Chickpea Salad, page 48), slaws (Crisp Cabbage Slaw, page 51), and bowls (Roasted Veg Quinoa Bowls, page 55). After giving it a good sear, the tuna is generously coated in roasted sesame seeds for a delightful nutty texture. Serve it up with a Ponzu Maple Vinaigrette or a simple ponzu.

1 tbsp neutral high-heat cooking oil, plus more for brushing the grill

¼ tsp kosher salt

Freshly cracked black pepper to taste

1 lb (450 g) fresh ahi tuna steaks (about 3)

¼ cup roasted black and white sesame seeds

Ponzu Maple Vinaigrette (page 28) or ponzu (see note)

1. Preheat the grill to medium-high heat (400°F/200°C). Make sure the grill is clean, then lightly brush the grid with oil.

2. Drizzle the oil over the tuna steaks and season with salt and pepper.

3. Grill the tuna using the crosshatch method, about 1 to 1½ minutes per flip, for a total of 4 to 6 minutes: Place the tuna steaks on a diagonal from the grids. On the first flip, maintain the same diagonal while turning the steaks over. On the next flip, rotate the steaks 180 degrees, to be on the opposite diagonal. On the last flip, maintain the second diagonal. You want the outside to be seared but for the center to still be pink.

4. Transfer the tuna to a cutting board. Fill a shallow dish with sesame seeds and dunk the steaks in the seeds to coat. Slice the tuna against the grain into thin pieces. Serve with ponzu maple vinaigrette.

NOTE

For a simple ponzu, mix together 2 tablespoons lemon juice, 2 tablespoons GF soy sauce or tamari, and 1 teaspoon mirin.

EASYGOING FLANK STEAK

SERVES 2 TO 4 🍴

Inspired by the book
Gathering around the Grill

♫ *Feel Good Inc – Gorillaz*

I could eat this versatile steak with just about everything. From salads to sandwiches, noodle bowls to rice bowls, it's ready to mingle! It's a recipe from my mother-in-law that I often crave, as it reminds me of breezy summer nights by the lake. Even though I'm usually a medium-rare kinda girl, I like to cook flank steak to medium, for a less chewy texture. A soy sauce marinade is a treat, since they're rarely gluten-free when not made at home, and the five-spice gives it that extra zhuzh to make it special. Plus, the lime juice in the marinade makes the meat extra tender. This recipe is best cooked on a grill, for optimal browning.

2 tbsp GF fish sauce

2 tbsp maple syrup

1 tbsp lime juice (about ½ lime)

½ tbsp GF soy sauce or tamari

½ tsp Chinese five-spice powder, or ¼ tsp ground cinnamon + ¼ tsp ground cloves

½ tsp garlic powder

1 tsp toasted sesame oil

1 tsp chili paste (such as sambal oelek or Calabrian)

2 lb (900 g) flank steak

Neutral high-heat cooking oil, for brushing the grill

1. In a large bowl, whisk together the fish sauce, maple syrup, lime juice, soy sauce, five-spice, garlic powder, sesame oil, and chili paste.

2. Using a chef's knife, score a crosshatch pattern on each side of the flank steak, to encourage browning when grilled. Make the scores no more than ¼ inch deep and at least 1 inch apart. Place the steak and marinade in a large storage bag, making sure the steak is submerged in the marinade. Marinate in the fridge for at least 30 minutes and up to 4 hours, flipping the bag occasionally.

3. Preheat the grill to medium-high heat (400°F/200°C). Make sure the grill is clean, then lightly brush the grid with cooking oil.

4. Grill the steak for about 4 minutes per side or until the internal temperature reaches 145°F (63°C) for medium. Transfer the steak to a cutting board, cover with foil, and let rest for 10 minutes before slicing against the grain.

CHILI CRISP HONEY RIBS

SERVES 8 TO 9

Inspired by
my BBQ-loving in-laws

♫ *Honeybody – Kishi Bashi*

I don't believe that pork ribs have to be falling off the bone to be considered good. These ribs strike the perfect balance—tender with a satisfying bite. They combine the homey flavors of Chinese BBQ pork and cha siu (which is rarely gluten-free), with the savory kick of chili crisp and the brightness of lime. It's an ideal dish for hosting friends and family, especially when served with a side of veg, like Sichuan-Style Charred Broccoli (page 173), and some steamed rice.

3 racks baby back ribs (about 5 lb/2.25 kg)

RUB

2 tsp kosher salt

⅓ cup packed brown sugar

1 tbsp garlic powder

2 tsp ground coriander (see note)

2 tsp mild paprika

1 tsp Chinese five-spice powder, or ½ tsp ground cinnamon + ½ tsp ground cloves

1 tsp ground ginger

GLAZE

¼ cup liquid honey

1 tbsp rice vinegar

½ tbsp GF soy sauce or tamari

½ tbsp chili crisp

¼ tsp cayenne

GARNISH (OPTIONAL)

Fresh cilantro and/or scallions, chopped

1 lime, cut into wedges

1. Preheat the grill or oven to 275°F (135°C). Line one baking sheet with foil. If using the oven, set aside a second baking sheet, leaving it unlined.

2. To remove the tough membrane from the ribs, lay a rack curved side up and slide a butter knife under the layer of white tissue between the first two bones. Wiggle the knife until the membrane becomes loose. Using a sheet of paper towel, grab the membrane and steadily peel it away from the ribs until the entire piece comes off. Discard and repeat with the other racks.

3. **MAKE THE RUB:** In a small bowl, combine the salt, brown sugar, garlic powder, coriander, paprika, five-spice, and ginger.

4. Generously rub the spice mixture on all sides of the ribs. Wrap each rack completely in foil.

5. If grilling, place the foil-wrapped ribs on the top rack of the grill or over an unlit burner with the other burners on. If roasting, place on the unlined pan on the middle oven rack. Grill, covered, or roast for 2 to 2½ hours, until the meat is tender and juicy.

6. **MAKE THE GLAZE:** In another small bowl, combine the honey, rice vinegar, soy sauce, chili crisp, and cayenne.

7. Unwrap the ribs. If roasting, transfer them to the lined baking sheet, or if grilling, make sure it's clean and place directly onto the grid. Bump the oven or grill temperature up to 400°F (200°C). Brush the glaze on the ribs, reserving 2 tablespoons. Roast for 30 minutes. If grilling, flip frequently until nicely browned. Transfer the racks to a cutting board and slice into individual ribs.

8. In a large bowl, toss the ribs with the remaining glaze. Transfer to a platter and, if using, serve garnished with cilantro, with lime wedges on the side.

NOTE

Toasting whole coriander and grinding it yourself will result in more flavorful ribs than using pre-ground coriander.

ROASTED CHICKEN LEGS WITH PHO BROTH GRAVY

Inspired by pho and holiday gatherings

♫ Manila – Maribou State

SERVES 4

This is my very North American version of chicken pho, featuring roasted chicken legs and richly thickened pho broth, without the actual pho (rice noodles). It brings me back to Thanksgiving at my aunt's when I was growing up, and what the occasion means for immigrant families, like my own, finding home in a new country. She made a triumphant effort, cooking all of the traditional Turkey Day dishes, always served alongside an array of Chinese takeout, a beautiful portrayal of the Chinese-Canadian experience. Dishes like these allow me to share my own journey and create new traditions. Serve with sides like Roasted Winter Squash with Nuoc Cham (page 169).

8 bone-in, skin-on chicken thighs, or 4 chicken legs (about 2.2 lb/1 kg)

2 tbsp neutral high-heat cooking oil

1 tsp kosher salt

1 tsp freshly cracked black pepper

1 tsp ground ginger

½ tsp fennel seeds

½ tsp coriander seeds

2 whole cloves

1 cinnamon stick, snapped in half

1 yellow onion, sliced into wedges

1 cup water

1 tbsp brown sugar or maple syrup

2 tbsp lime juice (about 1 lime)

2 tbsp GF fish sauce, soy sauce, or tamari

2 tsp cornstarch

2 tsp cool water

Fresh cilantro and/or basil (Thai or Italian), chopped

1 long red Thai chili, thinly sliced, or 2 tsp chili paste (such as sambal oelek or Calabrian)

1. Preheat the oven to 425°F (220°C)—ideally on the convection setting (but if you don't have that setting, you can use the broiler as described in step 6).

2. In a large bowl, combine the chicken with 1 tablespoon of the oil, salt, pepper, and ginger, tossing to coat evenly.

3. Place the fennel, coriander, cloves, and cinnamon in a tea bag to make a spice packet.

4. In a Dutch oven or ovenproof pot, heat the remaining oil on medium-high heat until it shimmers. Add the onion wedges and sear until browned and charred, about 3 minutes.

5. Reduce the heat to medium and stir in the water, brown sugar, lime juice, and fish sauce. Add the spice packet. Place the chicken in the pot, skin side up, making sure it is not fully submerged.

6. Transfer the pot to the oven and roast, uncovered, for 40 minutes or until the chicken is golden brown and no longer pink inside. If there's no convection setting on your oven and you'd like to brown the chicken more, broil on high on the top rack for the last 2 to 4 minutes. Using tongs, transfer the chicken to a dish.

7. Return the pot to the stovetop and reduce the sauce on medium heat for 5 minutes, stirring occasionally.

8. In a small bowl, mix the cornstarch with the cool water to make a slurry. Pour into the pot and simmer until the gravy is thickened. Discard the spice packet.

9. Serve the chicken drizzled with gravy and garnished with herbs and chilies.

NOTE

For convenience, instead of making the spice packet, you can include 1½ teaspoons of Chinese five-spice powder when seasoning the chicken.

STEAMED FISH EN PAPILLOTE

with Frizzled Ginger & Scallions

SERVES 2 TO 4

This recipe blends traditional Cantonese-style steamed whole fish with the "en papillote" technique of cooking in parchment paper that I learned in culinary school. Featuring delicately sweet sea bass and unexpected kalamata olives as a gluten-free alternative to fermented black beans, this dish is seasoned with fragrant frizzled ginger and scallions, plus a splash of soy sauce. Don't forget to savor the cheek—it's the best bite! My parents serve it to me and my sisters as the ultimate sign of affection.

1½ lb (675 g) whole sea bass or sea bream, scaled and cleaned at the store

1 tsp kosher salt

2 scallions, white and green parts separated, both cut into 2-inch segments, greens julienned

2-inch knob ginger, half sliced into diagonal cross-sections, half julienned

8 pitted kalamata olives

1 tbsp olive brine or water

1 tbsp extra virgin olive oil

2 tbsp neutral high-heat cooking oil

2 tbsp GF soy sauce or tamari

Fresh cilantro leaves (optional)

1. Preheat the oven to 425°F (220°C). Line a large baking sheet with a piece of parchment paper. Tear a second sheet of parchment paper the same size.

2. Place the fish on the prepared pan and rub both sides thoroughly with salt. Place the white scallions and ginger cross-sections in the cavity of the fish. Top the fish with the olives, olive brine, and olive oil. Place the second piece of parchment paper over the fish and fold the edges of both sheets to form an enclosed pouch.

3. Steam the wrapped fish ("en papillote") for 25 to 30 minutes, until it is opaque and flakes easily with a fork.

4. In a small frying pan, heat the cooking oil on medium-high heat until thin and shimmering, about 1 to 2 minutes.

5. Remove the top sheet of parchment paper. Top the fish with the julienned ginger and green scallions. Pour the hot oil over top. Drizzle with soy sauce and garnish with cilantro (if using). Serve directly from the baking sheet or carefully transfer the packet to a serving platter.

> **NOTE**
> Mama Lo tip: When picking out a whole fish at the store, choose the one with the glossiest eyes—that'll be the freshest one!

GLAZY PORK CHOPS WITH VERMICELLI

Inspired by
Vietnamese pork chop rice

♫ *Song – Sylvan Esso*

SERVES 4

As you may have noticed, I rely on a handful of ingredients in my cooking, and fish sauce is definitely a staple (we're so thankful it's gluten-free!). Paired with brown sugar, it creates a sweet and salty glaze that caramelizes beautifully when cooked. These pork chops are crave-worthy and embody everything pork chops should be—juicy, bursting with flavor, and served with fresh, bright ingredients for that sought-after balance.

4 cloves garlic, roughly sliced

2 small shallots, roughly sliced (about ¼ cup)

¼ cup packed brown sugar

¼ cup GF fish sauce

½ tsp freshly cracked black pepper

4 bone-in pork chops (about 1½ to 2 lb/675 to 900 g)

10½ oz (300 g) dried rice vermicelli

Neutral high-heat cooking oil, for brushing the grill and drizzling

Pickled Veg (page 25)

4 leaves crisp lettuce (such as romaine), chopped

¼ English cucumber, cut on a diagonal into ¼-inch slices

Fresh cilantro, scallions, mint, and/ or basil (Thai or Italian) leaves

Toasted peanuts (see page 25)

GF fried garlic or shallots

Lemony Nuoc Cham (page 30)

1. In a blender, combine the garlic, shallots, brown sugar, fish sauce, and pepper.

2. Place the pork chops in a large bowl, add the marinade, and toss to coat. Cover and marinate in the fridge for at least 30 minutes or up to overnight.

3. Meanwhile, in a large bowl, soak the vermicelli in cool water for at least 30 minutes.

4. Preheat the grill to medium-high heat (400°F/200°C). Make sure it's clean, then lightly brush the grid with oil.

5. Bring a large pot of salted water to a boil. Blanch the vermicelli until soft yet chewy, about 1 to 3 minutes. Check for doneness frequently. Drain the vermicelli in a colander and run under cold water. Drizzle with oil and toss to prevent clumping.

6. Meanwhile, pour the pork marinade into a small saucepan and bring to a simmer on medium-low heat. Simmer for 5 minutes, stirring occasionally.

7. Grill the pork chops, brushing them with the glazy marinade, for 3 to 4 minutes per side, until the internal temperature just reaches 145°F (63°C). If they are browning too quickly, transfer them to the top rack to cook on indirect heat. Transfer the pork chops to a plate or cutting board, cover with foil, and let rest for at least 5 minutes to kill off the bacteria.

8. Serve the pork chops with pickled veg, lettuce, cucumbers, herbs, peanuts, fried garlic, and vermicelli, and the nuoc cham on the side.

SWEET TREATS

Throughout various Asian cultures, desserts are all about enticing textures and subtle sweetness. They often incorporate a variety of naturally gluten-free flours, from glutinous rice flour to tapioca starch, which lend desserts the delightful, desirable springiness known as "QQ," not commonly found in Western cuisine. On the other hand, Western desserts are known for their decadence—in every way: I find they can occasionally be overly sweet and require laborious preparation.

The recipes in this chapter walk the line between both styles of dessert—because it's me, so we find balance in all things! Tailored to suit any level of expertise, this chapter showcases uncomplicated desserts that excel in both texture and flavor. Unlike many gluten-free baked goods, which end up dry and crumbly, the treats in this collection remain moist and pliable, like the craveable Banana Mochi Cake with Salted Coconut Cream (page 222).

With a nod to classic Western desserts, these recipes feature ingredients typical of traditional Asian treats, such as sesame and coconut, while also highlighting the freshness of seasonal fruits. Forget about complex pastry techniques; these are everyday recipes designed for anyone to whip up effortlessly. Personally, I'm all about preparing the Quick Macerated Berries with Mint & Coconut Whip (page 205) as an any-day treat, or baking a batch of Miso Tahini Cookies (page 226) to share with friends.

Scan me to
listen along!

QUICK MACERATED BERRIES

with Mint & Coconut Whip

SERVES 4 🐾 🌱 🍃

If you love fruit and coconut like I do, this one's for you. It's essentially a bowl of glossy, juicy berries, with a hint of mint for an unexpected herbal note, topped with coconut whip for a little decadence. A short maceration time with a sprinkle of sugar brings out the natural sweetness of the fruit without making it overly wet and mushy. Best with in-season, local berries! It's a simple pleasure that I could savor at the end of any meal in this book.

2 pints strawberries, raspberries, blackberries, and/or blueberries (24 oz/680 g)

1 tbsp granulated sugar or maple syrup

4 large mint leaves, finely chopped

1 canister (7.9 oz/225 g) coconut whip (see note)

1. If using strawberries, slice them. In a large bowl, use a spoon to toss the fruit with the sugar and mint. Let sit for 5 to 10 minutes.

2. Portion the fruit into bowls and top with coconut whip.

NOTE
Instead of canned coconut whip, you can refrigerate 1 can (14 oz/400 ml) full-fat coconut milk overnight, skim off the cream that forms on top, and whip it with 1 tablespoon of granulated sugar for 4 minutes in a stand mixer or with a hand mixer.

CORNMEAL MOCHI PANCAKES

with Macerated Berries & Coconut Whip

Inspired by cornbread

♫ *Keep Moving – Jungle*

MAKES 8 PANCAKES, SERVES 2 TO 4

This recipe combines two of my faves, cornbread and mochi, into delicious pancakes. The cornmeal adds a hint of sweetness, while the glutinous rice flour brings a nice light chew. Recommended additions include juicy Quick Macerated Berries with Mint & Coconut Whip (page 205) and a side of crisp, salty bacon for that delightful sweet and savory combo.

¾ cup (3.2 oz/90 g) glutinous rice flour

½ cup (2.7 oz/75 g) cornmeal

1 tbsp granulated sugar

1 tsp GF baking powder

½ tsp baking soda

¼ tsp kosher salt

1 large egg

½ cup whole milk

½ cup unsweetened plain yogurt (5%)

2 tbsp unsalted butter, melted

Coconut oil cooking spray or neutral cooking oil, for frying

Maple syrup, for serving

Quick Macerated Berries with Mint & Coconut Whip (page 205), for serving

1. In a large bowl, whisk together the rice flour, cornmeal, sugar, baking powder, baking soda, and salt.

2. In another large bowl, whisk together the egg, milk, yogurt, and butter. Add the cornmeal mixture and incorporate with a rubber spatula until uniform in consistency.

3. Preheat the oven to 150°F (65°C).

4. Heat a large nonstick frying pan on medium heat. Sprinkle a few drops of water on the pan; if it sizzles and evaporates quickly, it is ready. Spray or lightly oil the pan and reduce the heat to medium-low. Spoon in ¼ cup of batter and cook until small bubbles begin to form on top, about 3 minutes. Flip and cook until golden brown, about 2 minutes. Transfer to an ovenproof dish and keep warm in the oven. Repeat with the remaining batter.

5. Serve the pancakes with maple syrup and the macerated berries with coconut whip. Let extra pancakes cool on a wire rack and freeze for up to 1 month in a storage bag. Reheat frozen pancakes in a toaster until golden brown.

COCONUT MOCHI WAFFLES

Inspired by the springiness of
Hong Kong egg waffles

♫ *Can't Take My Eyes Off of You*
– Ms. Lauryn Hill

**MAKES 2 CIRCULAR WAFFLES,
OR ABOUT 3 RECTANGULAR WAFFLES**

This waffle recipe achieves the perfect harmony of crispy-chewy with a 1:1 ratio of white rice flour to glutinous rice flour. Despite its name, glutinous rice flour is 100% gluten-free: it's made of ground-up sticky rice. The key here is to use thick coconut cream as the liquid, for its richness, flavor, and ability to provide better structure to the waffles. I highly recommend serving these with pandan kaya, fresh fruits, and a dollop of coconut whip.

¾ cup (4.2 oz/120 g) white rice flour

¾ cup (3.2 oz/90 g) glutinous rice flour

½ cup (2.3 oz/64 g) tapioca starch

1 tbsp GF baking powder

½ tsp kosher salt

2 cups coconut cream (see note)

¼ cup (1.8 oz/50 g) packed brown sugar

2 tbsp neutral high-heat cooking oil, plus more for brushing

Pandan Kaya (page 31)

Powdered sugar, for dusting

Fresh fruits, for serving

PLANT-BASED OPTION

Pandan kaya → maple syrup

1. Preheat the waffle iron.

2. In a large bowl, whisk together the white rice flour, glutinous rice flour, tapioca starch, baking powder, and salt.

3. In another large bowl, whisk together the coconut cream, brown sugar, and oil. Slowly stir in the flour mixture until uniform in consistency. The batter will be thick.

4. Brush the top and bottom grids of the waffle iron with oil. Pour 1 cup of batter into the center, close, and cook until golden brown and crispy, about 5 to 7 minutes. Repeat with the remaining batter.

5. Serve the waffles with pandan kaya, dust with powdered sugar, and top with fresh fruits. Let extra waffles cool on a wire rack and freeze for up to 1 month in a storage bag. Reheat frozen waffles in a toaster until golden brown.

NOTE

If canned coconut cream is hard to find, you can refrigerate 2 cans (14 oz/400 ml each) of full-fat coconut milk for at least 30 minutes, skim off the top layer of cream that forms, and use that. Reserve the remaining coconut milk for rice, stews, or smoothies.

NUTTY SESAME GRANOLA

MAKES ABOUT 5 CUPS 🥄 🌱 🍃

A one-bowl, set-it-and-forget-it granola recipe is sure to be on frequent rotation for easygoing mornings at home. Infused with the comforting aroma of warm cinnamon and deeply nutty sesame oil—typically found in savory Asian dishes—this delicately sweet and crunchy version is perfect on top of yogurt with fresh-cut fruit, in smoothie bowls, over ice cream, or simply eaten by the handful as a snack.

2 cups GF large-flake rolled oats

½ cup large unsweetened coconut flakes

½ cup pumpkin or sunflower seeds

½ cup unsalted nuts (such as slivered almonds, chopped walnuts, or shelled pistachios)

¼ cup packed brown or coconut sugar

1 tbsp sesame seeds

½ tsp ground cinnamon

½ tsp kosher salt

¼ cup maple syrup

1 tbsp olive oil

1 tbsp toasted sesame oil

½ cup dried fruit (such as cranberries, raisins, currants, or chopped apricots or mangoes)

1. Preheat the oven to 350°F (180°C). Line a large baking sheet with parchment paper. (The pan should be large enough that the granola can be well spaced, to dry out and not form big clumps.)

2. In a bowl, combine all of the ingredients except the dried fruit and mix well with a rubber spatula. Spread out the granola mixture on the prepared pan.

3. Bake for 15 minutes. Turn off the oven. Remove the pan, stir and loosen up the granola into small clusters, and return to the oven to dry for 4 hours or up to overnight. Leave a sticky note on the oven door and set a timer so you don't forget!

4. Using your hands, break up granola clusters into smaller pieces. Combine with the dried fruit. Store in an airtight container at room temperature for up to 1 month.

NOTE
You can make this recipe at night and leave it in the oven to dehydrate while you sleep!

LIME LEAF SMOOTHIE BOWLS

SERVES 2 🐦 🌱 🍃

Inspired by hanging out with our Airbnb hosts in their café in Yogya

♫ *Light On – Maggie Rogers*

Kickstart the day on a high note with these special smoothie bowls. What sets them apart from the rest is the unexpected addition of makrut lime leaves. Just two leaves bring a burst of fresh, bright, and herbal flavors that takes the bowls to a new level. Top with Nutty Sesame Granola (page 210) and feel free to switch up the fixings.

2 cups frozen fruit

1 banana, roughly sliced

2 makrut lime leaves, stems removed, thinly sliced, or 1 tsp lime zest

½ cup GF oat milk (or milk of choice), plus more as needed

FIXINGS

Fresh fruits (such as sliced bananas, strawberries, mango, or kiwi, or whole blueberries, raspberries, or blackberries)

Nutty Sesame Granola (page 210)

Hemp or chia seeds

Toasted coconut flakes (see note)

Dried or fresh edible flowers

1. Place two serving bowls in the freezer.

2. In a blender, blitz the frozen fruit on the lowest setting to uniform tiny bits. Add the banana and lime leaves and pulse a few times, until combined. If needed, use a tamper to fully incorporate the ingredients. Add the oat milk and blend until thick and smooth, stopping and scraping down the sides with a rubber spatula as needed.

3. Portion the thick smoothie into the cooled serving bowls. Garnish with your fixings of choice. Serve immediately.

NOTE

Toast raw coconut flakes on medium heat for 3 to 4 minutes, until fragrant and golden, tossing frequently. Transfer to a plate and set aside to cool.

COCONUT SAGO PUDDING
with Watermelon

Inspired by Hong Kong dessert shops in Toronto

♫ *Ocean's Deep – Born Ruffians*

SERVES 4

This dessert brings me back to my one-month internship at a restaurant in Hong Kong just as I was wrapping up culinary school. After long days in the kitchen, I would anticipate stepping out into a refreshing breeze, only to be met with a wave of humid heat. Having grown up with Hong Kong–style dessert shops in Toronto, I knew to seek out treats like this refreshing coconut pudding after a kitchen shift, ordering in my heavily Canadian-accented Cantonese. My time in Hong Kong was an incredibly formative month of fully immersing myself in my culture.

½ cup sago pearls

1 can (14 oz/400 ml) full-fat coconut milk

3 tbsp granulated sugar

⅛ tsp kosher salt

¼ tsp vanilla extract

1 cup watermelon, cubed (see note)

1. Bring a small saucepan of water to a boil. Add the sago pearls and reduce the heat to medium, making sure to maintain a constant bubble. Cook the sago pearls for 10 minutes. Turn off the heat, cover, and let sit for 10 minutes, until the sago is transparent. Drain and set aside.

2. In another small saucepan, combine the coconut milk, sugar, salt, and vanilla. Heat on medium-low heat for 2 to 3 minutes, stirring until the sugar dissolves. Turn off the heat and stir in the cooked sago.

3. Prepare a bowl large enough to accommodate the saucepan by filling it with ice water. Dunk the bottom of the pan in the ice water to stop the pudding from cooking further.

4. Portion the pudding into jars or bowls and refrigerate until cold, about 1 hour. For a thicker consistency, let them sit in the fridge for an extra hour.

5. Serve garnished with the watermelon.

NOTE
My favorite topping is watermelon (bonus if you can find the yellow kind), but really, any fruit goes well over the coconut sago base.

MANGO CRISPY RICE

SERVES 2 🍸 ☘ 🌿

Inspired by mango sticky rice

♫ *Foreign Things*
– Amber Markt

One morning, I had a total aha moment while cutting up a mango and daydreaming about Thai mango sticky rice. If you're unfamiliar with the dessert, imagine the most beautiful golden mango slices paired with sticky rice and drizzled with a velvety, sweet coconut sauce. This recipe swaps out the sticky rice for gluten-free crispy rice cereal (silly that they aren't inherently gluten-free) and the coconut sauce with coconut yogurt, for a delightful twist on your standard yogurt and granola. First, find the ripest mango you can. Yellow Ataulfo are the best, IMO, since they're less fibrous. Look for a slightly wrinkled one that emits a powerful mango aroma—this will help you identify a ripe and super-tasty mango.

1 cup coconut-flavored yogurt

1 yellow (Ataulfo) mango, cubed

¼ cup GF crispy rice cereal (see note)

A drizzle of maple syrup

Toasted coconut flakes

DAIRY-FREE/PLANT-BASED OPTION

Coconut-flavored yogurt → coconut-based yogurt

1. In serving bowls, evenly portion out the yogurt, mango cubes, and crispy rice cereal. Drizzle maple syrup over top and garnish with a sprinkling of coconut flakes.

NOTES

You might think all crispy rice cereals are gluten-free, since rice is, but they are often created with gluteny grain products like barley malt extract, so be sure to check the ingredients list. Nature's Path has a reliable gluten-free crispy rice cereal.

If you can find those little mochi bites they serve at frozen yogurt shops, add them for the ultimate mango crispy-chewy rice!

BLACK SESAME BUTTERMILK LOAF

Inspired by Poh's glutinous rice dumplings (tang yuan)

♪ 6's to 9's (feat. Rationale) – Big Wild

MAKES 9 SQUARES 🥕 🌿

Here's a treat that hits the spot with your morning coffee or afternoon tea, or as a post-dinner dessert. Reminiscent of Poh's tang yuan filling, the toasty ground black sesame shines through in this airy loaf, that's delightfully nutty and not too sweet.

Unsalted butter, neutral cooking oil, or cooking spray, for greasing

⅓ cup (1.8 oz/50 g) toasted black sesame seeds

1¼ cups (5.3 oz/150 g) GF all-purpose flour

1 tsp GF baking powder

¾ tsp kosher salt

¼ tsp baking soda

¼ tsp xanthan gum (see note)

½ cup + 2 tbsp (4.4 oz/125 g) granulated sugar

2 large eggs

½ cup buttermilk

¼ cup + 2 tbsp (3 oz/85 g) unsalted butter, melted and cooled

2 tbsp neutral cooking oil

1 tsp vanilla extract

1. Preheat the oven to 350°F (180°C). Grease an 8-inch square pan and line it with a sheet of parchment paper the width of the bottom of the pan and long enough to overhang two sides. (You'll use the edges to pull out the baked loaf.)

2. In a small blender, spice grinder, or mortar and pestle, pulverize the sesame seeds into a fine powder.

3. In a medium bowl, whisk together the sesame powder, flour, baking powder, salt, baking soda, and xanthan gum.

4. In a large bowl, whisk the sugar, eggs, buttermilk, butter, oil, and vanilla until uniform in consistency. Add the flour mixture and mix until smooth. Pour the batter into the prepared pan.

5. Bake for 27 to 30 minutes, until a toothpick comes out with some moist crumbs. Let cool for 15 minutes in the pan, then use the overhanging parchment to lift the loaf onto a wire rack until cool to touch. Cut into nine squares and store in an airtight container for up to 3 days at room temperature, or up to 1 week in the fridge. Gently warm a loaf from the fridge in the microwave for 10 to 15 seconds.

NOTE
If your GF all-purpose flour includes xanthan gum, decrease the amount of xanthan gum in this recipe by half.

YUZU SQUARES

Inspired by Granny Hill

♫ *Sir Duke – Stevie Wonder*

MAKES 16 SMALL SQUARES 🥕 🌿

These decadent yuzu squares are inspired by my late grandmother-in-law's cherished lemon squares. In place of lemon, I've used yuzu, an extremely fragrant citrus fruit from Japan—reminiscent in scent of lemons, mandarins, and grapefruit—as another way to consume this spectacularly bright-tasting fruit. I often use bottled yuzu juice from specialty Japanese markets, but if you can't find it, lemon juice mixed with grapefruit zest will still yield a delightful result!

CRUST

Unsalted butter, neutral cooking oil, or cooking spray, for greasing

1 cup (4.2 oz/120 g) GF all-purpose flour

¼ cup (1.1 oz/32 g) icing sugar

¼ tsp kosher salt

½ cup (4 oz/113 g) unsalted butter, at room temperature (see note)

YUZU FILLING

1 cup (7.1 oz/200 g) granulated sugar

2 tbsp GF all-purpose flour

2 large eggs

¼ cup fresh or bottled yuzu juice

Zest of 1 lemon

Icing sugar, for dusting

SUB

If you can't find yuzu juice, replace it with lemon juice and substitute the zest of ⅓ grapefruit for the lemon zest.

1. **MAKE THE CRUST:** Preheat the oven to 350°F (180°C). Grease an 8-inch square pan and line it with two sheets of parchment paper the width of the bottom of the pan and long enough to overhang the sides. (You want to ensure that the yuzu filling doesn't stick to the sides, and you'll use the edges to pull out the baked, uncut square.)

2. In a large bowl, combine the flour, icing sugar, salt, and butter. Use a fork to break up the butter into smaller chunks, then use your hands to form the dough into small clumps (you're not looking for a consistent or smooth texture here). Firmly pat the dough into an even layer into the prepared pan. Refrigerate for 5 minutes.

3. Bake for 22 to 24 minutes, until the edges of the pastry are the color of creamy coffee.

4. **MAKE THE YUZU FILLING:** Meanwhile, in a large bowl, whisk together the sugar, flour, eggs, yuzu juice, and lemon zest.

5. Pour the filling into the crust and bake for 20 to 22 minutes, until fully set. Let cool in the pan on a wire rack for 1 hour, then transfer the pan to the fridge for 30 minutes.

6. Use the overhanging parchment to lift the square onto a cutting board. Using a fine-mesh sieve, dust icing sugar over top. Slice into 16 squares. Store in an airtight container in the fridge for up to 1 week.

NOTE

The best hack for getting room temperature butter without planning ahead is to microwave butter from the fridge for 10 to 15 seconds. Keep an eye on it as it's warming up—don't let it melt!

BANANA MOCHI CAKE
with Salted Coconut Cream

Inspired by the smell of banana bread wafting through the house

♫ *Cheap Sunglasses (feat. Matthew Koma) - RAC*

MAKES 24 SMALL SQUARES

For events—or really, in general—people go wild over layer cakes, but if I'm honest, making them really isn't my jam. They just don't light me up the way this humble banana mochi cake does. It's reminiscent of my sister's banana bread, with its intoxicatingly sweet, caramelly aroma that instantly boosts my mood. My cake has a light chew, 'cause I love me some mochi, and it's drenched in a decadently warm salted coconut cream. Plus, I sprinkle on some dried edible flowers to make it extra spesh—perfect for birthdays or just because.

BANANA MOCHI CAKE

Unsalted butter, neutral cooking oil, or cooking spray, for greasing

2 cans (14 oz/400 mL each) full-fat coconut milk

1 tbsp white vinegar

2 cups (8.5 oz/240 g) GF all-purpose flour

1 cup (4.2 oz/120 g) glutinous rice flour

1 tsp baking soda

1 tsp GF baking powder

½ tsp ground cinnamon

½ tsp kosher salt

1 cup (7.1 oz/200 g) granulated sugar

½ cup (3.5 oz/100 g) packed brown sugar

¾ cup (6 oz/170 g) unsalted butter, at room temperature (see note on page 221)

3 large eggs

3 ripe bananas, peeled and mashed (12.2 oz/345 g)

1 tsp vanilla extract

SALTED COCONUT CREAM

2 tbsp granulated sugar

A pinch of kosher salt

4 tsp cornstarch

4 tsp cool water

Dried edible flowers, to garnish

1. **MAKE THE CAKE:** Preheat the oven to 350°F (180°C). Grease a 9×13-inch baking pan and line it with a sheet of parchment paper the width of the bottom of the pan and long enough to overhang the short sides. (You'll use the edges to pull out the baked loaf.)

2. In a small bowl, stir together 1½ cups of the coconut milk with the vinegar and set aside for 5 minutes.

3. Meanwhile, in a large bowl, whisk together the all-purpose flour, glutinous rice flour, baking soda, baking powder, cinnamon, and salt.

4. In a stand mixer bowl with the paddle attachment or another large bowl with a hand mixer, cream together the granulated sugar, brown sugar, and butter on medium-low speed for 2 minutes, until pale yellow and just uniform in consistency. Beat in the eggs, bananas, and vanilla. Slowly pour in the coconut milk mixture until just combined. Add the dry ingredients and mix until a uniform batter has formed.

5. Pour the batter into the prepared pan, scraping the bowl with a rubber spatula.

6. Bake for 45 to 50 minutes, until a toothpick inserted in the center comes out clean. Transfer the pan to a wire rack and let cool in the pan for 1 hour.

7. **MAKE THE SALTED COCONUT CREAM:** Right before serving the cake, in a small saucepan, heat the remaining coconut milk with the sugar and a good pinch of salt over medium heat until steaming.

8. In a small bowl, mix the cornstarch with the cool water to make a slurry. Pour into the pan and heat, stirring, until the coconut cream has thickened. Remove from the heat.

9. Use the overhanging parchment to lift the cake onto a cutting board. Cut the cake into 24 small squares. Drizzle with salted coconut cream and garnish with edible flowers.

MATCHA WHITE CHOCOLATE CHIP COOKIES

MAKES ABOUT 24 COOKIES 🥕 🌿

Inspired by matcha lattes

♫ *If We Want To – M.I.L.K.*

It's hard to believe these cookies are gluten-free, given their ideal texture: perfectly crisp on the outside and chewy on the inside, making it impossible to stop at just one. White chocolate chips provide delicate sweetness to contrast the earthy, bittersweet matcha. They're the perfect pick-me-up and pair well with a glass of milk.

2 cups (8.5 oz/240 g) GF all-purpose flour

1½ tbsp matcha powder

1 tsp xanthan gum (see note, page 218)

1 tsp baking soda

½ tsp kosher salt

¾ cup (5.3 oz/150 g) granulated sugar

½ cup (3.5 oz/100 g) brown sugar

½ cup (4 oz/113 g) unsalted butter, microwaved for 5 seconds

2 large eggs

1½ tsp vanilla extract

1 bag (8 oz/225 g) white chocolate chips

1. In a large bowl, whisk together the flour, matcha powder, xanthan gum, baking soda, and salt.

2. In a stand mixer with the paddle attachment or another large bowl with a hand mixer, cream together the granulated sugar, brown sugar, and butter on low speed for 2 minutes, until beige and just uniform in consistency. Add the eggs and vanilla and mix until just incorporated. Do not overmix or the mixture will curdle. Add the flour mixture, one-third at a time, mixing a little between each addition. After the last addition, mix until a playdough-like dough forms. Add the white chocolate chips and mix to combine.

3. Chill the dough in the freezer for 20 minutes, until it feels like playdough. You may be tempted to skip this step, but it will keep your cookies from melting together while baking.

4. Preheat the oven to 350°F (180°C). Line two baking sheets with parchment paper.

5. Form the dough into heaping tablespoon–sized balls. Space out the balls on the prepared pans in four rows of three. Flatten the balls slightly with your fingertips.

6. Bake, one pan at a time (see note, page 226), for 14 to 17 minutes, until just cooked through and still slightly soft to touch. Let cool on the pan for 5 minutes, then gently transfer the cookies to a wire rack and let cool until firm.

7. Store in an airtight container at room temperature for up to 1 week, or freeze (see note).

NOTE

You can easily divide the raw dough into halves or thirds to freeze flat in large freezer bags for up to 2 months, perfect to have on hand to bake on a rainy day. Simply thaw it for 24 hours in the fridge, then form the dough into balls. You can also freeze the baked cookies and defrost them at room temperature. Throughout the week, microwave room-temperature cookies for about 10 to 15 seconds for a fresh-out-of-the-oven experience.

MISO TAHINI COOKIES

MAKES ABOUT 24 COOKIES 🥕 🌿

Inspired by
peanut butter cookies

♫ *CUFF IT – Beyoncé*

What is it that's so inspiring when the sun goes down? Because sometimes I get the urge to bake at 9 p.m. These cookies are a go-to, since they're relatively quick from start to finish, especially if it's a binge-TV type of night. They're salty from the miso, nutty from the tahini, and totally addictive. Sticking the dough in the freezer for 20 minutes before baking gives it the ideal crispy-chewy texture and prevents the cookies from spreading into one giant cookie.

1½ cups (6.3 oz/180 g) GF all-purpose flour

1 tsp xanthan gum (see note, page 218)

1 tsp baking soda

1 cup (7.1 oz/200 g) packed brown sugar

½ cup (4 oz/113 g) unsalted butter, microwaved for 5 seconds

1 large egg

¼ cup GF miso paste

¼ cup tahini, at room temperature

1½ tsp vanilla extract

¼ cup (1.8 oz/50 g) granulated sugar, or as needed

Roasted sesame seeds

1. In a large bowl, whisk together the flour, xanthan gum, and baking soda.

2. In a stand mixer with the paddle attachment or another large bowl with a hand mixer, cream together the brown sugar and butter on medium-low speed for 2 minutes, until pale yellow and just uniform in consistency. Add the egg, miso, tahini, and vanilla and mix until just incorporated. Do not overmix or the mixture will curdle. Add the flour mixture, one-third at a time, mixing a little between each addition. After the last addition, mix until a playdough-like dough forms.

3. Chill the dough in the freezer for 20 minutes, until it feels like playdough. You may be tempted to skip this step, but it will keep your cookies from melting together while baking.

4. Preheat the oven to 350°F (180°C). Line two baking sheets with parchment paper.

5. Form the dough into heaping tablespoon-sized balls. Roll the balls in the granulated sugar until evenly coated. Space out the balls on the prepared pans in four rows of three. Use a fork to flatten each cookie slightly and make crosshatch marks on top. Sprinkle with sesame seeds.

6. Bake, one pan at a time (see note), for 12 to 16 minutes, until just cooked through and still slightly soft to the touch. Let cool on the pan for 5 minutes, then gently transfer the cookies to a wire rack and let cool until firm.

7. Store in an airtight container at room temperature for up to 1 week, or freeze (see note on page 225).

NOTES

I recommend baking the pans one at a time on the middle rack, but if you want to bake both at once, place one rack in the top third and one rack in the bottom third of the oven before preheating it. When the oven is preheated, place one pan on the top rack and one on the bottom, then switch their positions halfway through baking.

PANDAN KAYA FRENCH TOAST

Inspired by
Singaporean kaya toast

♫ *Marche, Pt. 2 – Moi Je*

SERVES 2 🐦 🥕 🌿

This is my spin on a Singaporean classic: kaya toast. Instead of maple syrup, I serve French toast with pandan kaya, a spreadable coconut custard infused with pandan, which has complex caramel and herbal notes and is sometimes called "Asia's vanilla" for its complex, nutty flavor and prominence in Southeast Asian desserts.

1 large egg

¼ cup whole milk

1 tsp brown sugar or maple syrup

A pinch of kosher salt

4 slices GF bread

1 tbsp unsalted butter, plus more for serving

Pandan Kaya (page 31 or store-bought)

DAIRY-FREE OPTION

• Whole milk → unsweetened non-dairy milk

• Butter → neutral high-heat cooking oil

1. In a large bowl, whisk together the egg, milk, brown sugar, and salt.

2. In a large nonstick frying pan, melt the butter on medium heat. Working in batches as needed, dunk the bread in the egg mixture, coating both sides evenly. Fry until golden brown, about 2 to 3 minutes per side.

3. Serve the French toast topped with butter and pandan kaya.

NOTE

Our top choices for sliced gluten-free bread brands are Promise, Little Northern Bakehouse, Canyon Bakehouse, and Schär. If your bread is frozen, toast it until just defrosted and soft before proceeding with step 2.

PAVLOVA WITH CALAMANSI CURD

SERVES 8 🐟 🥕 🌿

Inspired by Reid's birthdays
♫ *Moth's Wings – Passion Pit*

Crisp on the outside and soft on the inside, pavlova is a naturally gluten-free treat that has brought consistent joy to Reid's birthdays year after year. In this version, the airy and sweet meringue serves as the perfect canvas for tart and floral calamansi curd, made from the popular Filipino citrus. An array of fresh fruits adds another dimension of excitement to the dessert.

MERINGUE

4 large egg whites

¼ tsp kosher salt

¼ tsp cream of tartar

1 cup (7.1 oz/200 g) granulated sugar

4 tsp cornstarch

2 tsp white vinegar

1 tsp vanilla extract

CALAMANSI CURD

⅔ cup (4.7 oz/133 g) granulated sugar

1 tbsp lime zest

½ cup calamansi juice, lemon juice, or lime juice (see note)

4 large eggs

Fresh fruits of choice (I like berries and sliced mangoes, peaches, and kiwis)

1. **MAKE THE MERINGUE:** Preheat the oven to 250°F (120°C). Line a baking sheet with parchment paper.

2. In a stand mixer with the whisk attachment or a large bowl with a hand mixer, beat the egg whites, salt, and cream of tartar until the whites hold stiff peaks. Add the sugar, a few tablespoons at a time, beating until stiff and glossy. Add the cornstarch, vinegar, and vanilla and beat until well combined.

3. Spread the meringue mixture onto the prepared pan into two circles or one large oval, about 1½ inches thick, with the edges slightly higher than the middle, forming a depression.

4. Bake for 1 hour, until the meringue is firm and barely browned. Turn off the oven and leave the meringue inside for 1 hour (this step is crucial and should not be rushed). Remove from the oven and let cool completely.

5. **MEANWHILE, MAKE THE CALAMANSI CURD:** In a medium saucepan, combine the sugar, lime zest, and calamansi juice. Bring to a boil, then turn off the heat.

6. In a medium bowl, beat the eggs. Place a damp rag under the bowl to keep it from wobbling and, whisking constantly, slowly pour in the calamansi syrup until completely incorporated.

7. Return the mixture to the pan and cook, whisking constantly, on medium-low heat for 3 to 5 minutes or until the curd reaches the consistency of mayo.

8. Strain the curd into a clean bowl and chill in the fridge until cool (or cover and store in the fridge for up to 1 week).

9. Gently transfer the meringue to a serving platter. Coat the meringue with the calamansi curd over the surface and top with fresh fruits.

NOTE

Freeze the egg yolks left over from the meringue for up to 3 months. Thaw them in the fridge for 24 hours to make Miso Crème Brûlée (page 233)!

Calamansi juice can be found at your local East or Southeast Asian market, specialty food store, or large supermarket.

MISO CRÈME BRÛLÉE

SERVES 4 TO 6 🐷 🥕 🌿

Inspired by a miso custard
dessert at NOPI in London

♫ *Need Your Love*
– Curtis Harding

My best culinary creations come from working with limitations. Put me in an *Iron Chef* showdown with leftovers, and I'd shine brighter than with an unlimited pantry. This dairy-free crème brûlée is another Monty's pop-up creation for a vegetarian night I hosted. The miso brings out a rich, salty-sweet custard that'll totally fool you into believing it's loaded with dairy. I love a sweet and savory dessert. Garnish it with some tart berries or juicy peaches for a good richness-to-brightness ratio. You're going to need a kitchen torch for this (borrow one from a foodie friend if you don't want to buy one). My top pick for power and price is a torch head that can be directly attached to a butane canister.

1 can (14 oz/400 mL) full-fat coconut milk

1½ tbsp GF miso paste

1 tsp vanilla extract

5 large egg yolks

¾ cup (5.3 oz/150 g) granulated sugar, plus more for topping

Sliced berries or stone fruit, for serving

Mint leaves, to garnish

1. Preheat the oven to 325°F (165°C).

2. In a small saucepan, heat the coconut milk, miso, and vanilla on medium-low heat, whisking to combine, until the miso has dissolved; do not boil. Set aside to cool to room temperature.

3. In a medium bowl, whisk together the egg yolks and sugar. Place a damp rag under the bowl to keep it from wobbling and, whisking constantly, slowly pour in the cooled cream mixture until completely incorporated.

4. Place four to six small ramekins in a deep baking dish and divide the custard mixture among the ramekins. Add warm water to the baking dish until it reaches halfway up the sides of the ramekins.

5. Bake for 45 to 55 minutes. To check that the custard is done, gently shake the baking dish to check that the center of the custard no longer jiggles. With a kitchen towel or oven mitts, transfer the ramekins to a wire rack and let cool for at least 15 minutes or until cool enough to touch.

6. Sprinkle a thin layer of sugar on top of each custard, tilting the ramekins to make sure it is evenly distributed. Fire up a kitchen torch and caramelize the sugar until beautifully browned. Top with fruit and mint.

NOTE
The cooked custard can be kept in the fridge, covered, for up to 2 days, until you're ready to torch and serve it.

BRINGING PEOPLE TOGETHER
MENUS

One of my greatest joys is creating memorable moments through food, so I've put together a few menus to help you to do the same.

AL FRESCO DINING
Any reason to eat outside when it's nice out, am I right?

- Peak Summer Salad with Burrata & Dumpling Sauce (page 43)
- Cha Siu Chicken Sandos with Sesame Chili Mayo (page 186)
- Grilled Veg with Gomae (page 174)
- Yuzu Squares (page 221)

OR

- Herbaceous Melon Salad with Bacon & Nuoc Cham Vinaigrette (page 40)
- Easygoing Flank Steak (page 193)
- Grilled Corn with Kimchi Shrimp Mayo (page 178)
- Coconut Sago Pudding with Watermelon (page 214)

COZY HOLIDAY FEASTS
Warm the belly and soul with these cold-weather faves.

- Tender Kale, Asian Pear & Roasted Butternut Squash with Feta & Fried Shallot Dressing (page 56)
- Vietnamese Short Rib Stew (page 101)
- Sichuan-Style Charred Broccoli (page 173)
- Banana Mochi Cake with Salted Coconut Cream (page 222)

OR

- Orange & Asian Pear Slaw with Lemony Nuoc Cham (page 36)
- Massaman Beef Curry with Baby Potatoes (page 97)
- Caramelized Chili Maple Carrots with Thai Basil Pesto (page 170)
- Miso Crème Brûlée (page 233)

LET'S CELEBRATE!

For celebrating life's big and small occasions!

- Summer Rolls with Ssamjang (page 65)
- Birthday Crab (page 125)
- Pavlova with Calamansi Curd (page 230)

OR

- Smacked Cucumber Salad (page 63)
- Gochujang-Braised Pork Shoulder & Fixings (page 102)
- Quick Macerated Berries with Mint & Coconut Whip (page 205)

AN EXTRAVAGANT FAMILY-STYLE SPREAD

A feast for larger groups!
(photo spread on page 236)

- Tomatoes with Feta & Scallion Ginger Oil (page 35)
- Crisp Cabbage Slaw (page 51)
- Hot & Sour Soup (page 88)
- Grilled Corn with Kimchi Shrimp Mayo (page 178)
- Chili Crisp Honey Ribs (page 194)
- Chili Miso Salmon (page 182)
- Birthday Crab (page 125)

LUNAR NEW YEAR

An array of auspicious dishes to ring in the new year!

- Smacked Cucumber Salad (page 63)
- Roasted Coconut Tamari Chicken (page 114) *or* Five-Spice Duck Breast with Scallion Crepes (page 142) *or* Steamed Fish en Papillote with Frizzled Ginger & Scallions (page 198)
- Pork & Watercress Crystal Dumplings (page 155) *or* Stir-Fried Rice Noodles with Sausage & Bean Sprouts (page 145) *or* Fried Rice Formula (page 136)
- The Ideal Stir-Fry (page 135)
- Coconut Sago Pudding with Watermelon (page 214)

PLANT-BASED SPREADS

Veg-happy spreads for veg-happy people.

- Charred Romaine with Silken Tofu Caesar Dressing (page 59, plant-based option)
- Miso ~~Cream of~~ Mushroom Soup (page 84, plant-based option)
- Shanghai Stir-Fried Gnocchi (page 148, plant-based option)
- Coconut Mochi Waffles (page 209)

OR

- Flavor Bomb Edamame (page 39)
- Roasted Cauliflower with Spicy Miso Tahini & Garlicky Panko (page 177)
- Japanese-Style Curry (page 113, plant-based option)
- Lime Leaf Smoothie Bowls (page 213)

DIETARY LISTS

🐟 DAIRY-FREE

141	Cabbage Pancakes with Scallions & Yum Yum Sauce	181	Miso Cod with Oyster Mushrooms & Bok Choy
142	Five-Spice Duck Breast with Scallion Crepes (dairy-free option)	182	Chili Miso Salmon
145	Stir-Fried Rice Noodles with Sausage & Bean Sprouts	185	Caramelized Sweet Chili Shrimp
147	Pork & Basil Stir-Fry with Crispy Fried Eggs	186	Cha Siu Chicken Sandos with Sesame Chili Mayo
148	Shanghai Stir-Fried Gnocchi	189	Gochujang Chicken Wings
151	Minced Pork Noodles with Cucumbers	190	Sesame Tuna Steaks with Ponzu
152	Chicken Thigh Katsu	193	Easygoing Flank Steak
155	Pork & Watercress Crystal Dumplings	194	Chili Crisp Honey Ribs
159	Salmon Burgers with Sesame Chili Mayo	197	Roasted Chicken Legs with Pho Broth Gravy
160	Coconut Lime Shrimp Pasta with Parm (dairy-free option)	198	Steamed Fish en Papillote with Frizzled Ginger & Scallions
163	Frizzled Sardine Rice with Fried Crispy Eggs	201	Glazy Pork Chops with Vermicelli
169	Roasted Winter Squash with Nuoc Cham	205	Quick Macerated Berries with Mint & Coconut Whip
170	Caramelized Chili Maple Carrots with Thai Basil Pesto	209	Coconut Mochi Waffles
173	Sichuan-Style Charred Broccoli	210	Nutty Sesame Granola
174	Grilled Veg with Gomae	213	Lime Leaf Smoothie Bowls
177	Roasted Cauliflower with Spicy Miso Tahini & Garlicky Panko	214	Coconut Sago Pudding with Watermelon
178	Grilled Corn with Kimchi Shrimp Mayo	217	Mango Crispy Rice (dairy-free option)
		229	Pandan Kaya French Toast (dairy-free option)
		230	Pavlova with Calamansi Curd
		233	Miso Crème Brûlée

PLANT-BASED

35	Tomatoes with Feta & Scallion Ginger Oil (plant-based option)	48	Tuna & Curry-Roasted Chickpea Salad with Ponzu Maple Vinaigrette (plant-based option)
36	Orange & Asian Pear Slaw with Lemony Nuoc Cham (plant-based option)	51	Crisp Cabbage Slaw
39	Flavor Bomb Edamame	52	Charred Corn Salad with Coconut Cream
40	Herbaceous Melon Salad with Bacon & Nuoc Cham Vinaigrette (plant-based option)	55	Roasted Veg Quinoa Bowls with Lemon Ginger Vinaigrette
43	Peak Summer Salad with Burrata & Dumpling Sauce (plant-based option)	56	Tender Kale, Asian Pear & Butternut Squash with Feta & Fried Shallot Dressing (plant-based option)
44	Silken Tofu Salad with Tamari & Scallion Ginger Oil	59	Charred Romaine with Silken Tofu Caesar Dressing (plant-based option)
		60	Magic Spuds Salad (plant-based option)

❦ VEGETARIAN

(The following recipes contain eggs; all of the plant-based recipes listed above are, of course, vegetarian as well)

88	Hot & Sour Soup
121	Tomato, Egg & Pesto Stir-Fry (vegetarian option)
122	Fish Sauce Oyakodon (vegetarian option)
132	'Shroom Toast with Chili Miso
136	Fried Rice Formula (vegetarian option)
141	Cabbage Pancakes with Scallions & Yum Yum Sauce
147	Pork & Basil Stir-Fry with Crispy Fried Eggs (vegetarian option)

155	Pork & Watercress Crystal Dumplings (vegetarian option)
206	Cornmeal Mochi Pancakes with Macerated Berries & Coconut Whip
218	Black Sesame Buttermilk Loaf
221	Yuzu Squares
222	Banana Mochi Cake with Salted Coconut Cream
225	Matcha White Chocolate Chip Cookies
226	Miso Tahini Cookies
229	Pandan Kaya French Toast
230	Pavlova with Calamansi Curd
233	Miso Crème Brûlée

🌿 PESCATARIAN

35	Tomatoes with Feta & Scallion Ginger Oil
36	Orange & Asian Pear Slaw with Lemony Nuoc Cham
39	Flavor Bomb Edamame
40	Herbaceous Melon Salad with Bacon & Nuoc Cham Vinaigrette (plant-based option)
43	Peak Summer Salad with Burrata & Dumpling Sauce
44	Silken Tofu Salad with Tamari & Scallion Ginger Oil
47	Coconut Lime Ceviche with Golden Kiwi
48	Tuna & Curry-Roasted Chickpea Salad with Ponzu Maple Vinaigrette
51	Crisp Cabbage Slaw
52	Charred Corn Salad with Coconut Cream
55	Roasted Veg Quinoa Bowls with Lemon Ginger Vinaigrette
56	Tender Kale, Asian Pear & Roasted Butternut Squash with Feta & Fried Shallot Dressing
59	Charred Romaine with Silken Tofu Caesar Dressing
60	Magic Spuds Salad

63	Smacked Cucumber Salad
65	Summer Rolls with Ssamjang
71	Tom Yum Corn Chowder
72	Rice Cake Soup with Ground Pork & Spinach (plant-based option)
75	Coconut Curry Noodle Soup (plant-based option)
76	Sweet Potato & Cauliflower Purée with Chinese Sausage (plant-based option)
79	Turmeric & Rice Chicken Soup (plant-based option)
80	Quick Miso (Noodle) Soup
83	Macaroni Laksa
84	Miso Cream of Mushroom Soup
87	Turmeric & Dill Soup with Sausage, Potato & Kale (plant-based option)
88	Hot & Sour Soup
91	Pumpkin, Corn & White Fish Congee
92	Peanutty Rainbow Chard & Sweet Potato Chowder
98	Spicy Korean-Style Seafood Stew
106	Canto-Style Mapo Tofu (plant-based option)

ACKNOWLEDGMENTS

I can hardly believe I'm at the stage where I'm wrapping up my manuscript and preparing to release my book baby into the world. This journey has been a wild ride of invaluable lessons, and I'm immensely grateful to everyone who helped bring my dream project to fruition.

This book was sparked by a conversation with my dear friend and photographer, Jess Kalman. Jess, you've had my back since day one—your encouragement gave me the push I needed to start, and here we freaking are! You're the best work buddy a girl could ask for, from running out for last-minute ingredients and volunteering to test recipes to taking a month off from your day job for the shoots. May 2023 was a whirlwind, but we had a blast, and I can't thank you enough for the time and energy you've given me.

Shortly after that conversation with Jess, I found my book coach, Amanda Polick, through the Cherry Bombe community. (Thanks, Bombe Squad!) She eased my doubts, answered all my questions, and guided me in crafting an incredibly solid book proposal that led to my book deal. Amanda, thank you for believing in me from the start and helping me uncover my "why." I'm so happy our paths crossed; I don't know what this process would have looked like without you.

When I first heard back from Appetite (pinch me, am I really publishing with an imprint of Penguin Random House Canada?!), I couldn't believe their enthusiasm. When your prospective publisher and editor read through your entire body of work and acknowledge the effort you've put in, you know it was meant to be. Thank you to my publisher, Robert McCullough, for your commitment to my vision. And thank you Whitney Millar, for grasping the essence of what I

wanted to communicate, the thorough edits, the flexible coordination for design, and the countless hours of work beyond the manuscript. I couldn't have asked for a more aligned editor who has my back. To Dylan Browne, Lindsay Paterson, and the rest of the team at Appetite, your hard work and dedication have made this dream a reality for me, and I'm beyond ecstatic with the outcome.

Thank you to my dear sister Janet Lo, the creative force and mama bear behind the photo shoots. I have so much gratitude for our lengthy planning calls, your cross-continent journey home for the shoots, and the massive Chinatown props haul you orchestrated for the cause. You taught Jess and me so much about food styling, and we wouldn't have been able to bring my "jungle boo" vision to life without your keen eye and guidance.

Thank you also to my dear sister Joannza Lo, for joining the creative team at the eleventh hour and going above and beyond on page illustration samples across time zones from Korea to Toronto. Your dedication, time, and energy, especially under such a tight deadline, mean the world to me. I'm so happy this became a sister project; it was a joy collaborating with you both.

A heartfelt thanks to the talented Nancy Pappas for the awesome pantry illustrations. Our connection through Dump the Hate brought us together from across borders, and despite that distance, you are a dear friend to me.

To my community, Instagram network, and recipe testers, I'm so thrilled that you've joined me on this journey. The recipes in this book are dedicated to you, with the aim of nourishing and uniting through dishes that hold a special place in my heart. Your support over the years has not gone unnoticed, and I'm so excited to share gluten-free Asian cooking insights with you through this book. Special thanks to Theresa Hillis for testing every recipe I sent your way, without fail.

Thank you to the chefs and food creators who have been and continue to be an inspiration to me daily, and to Joie Alvaro Kent for your generosity and food writing insights.

Mom, Dad, my sisters, and my extended family, you are my heart and driving force. My love of food stems from you, and I love you deeply. Gong and Poh, though our time together was brief, the early food memories we shared remain ingrained in me. I wish I could cook for you and show you who I've become, but I feel your presence with me always.

To my dear in-laws and second extended family, thank you for embracing me with open arms and sharing your lives with me. The delicious meals we've created together have influenced many recipes in this book, and I can't wait to make more.

My friends! I hold each of you close. Thank you for your constant support and for listening to me talk about this project for the past few years. It's finally here!

And last but not least, Reid. Our shared experiences have ultimately led to this book, and I love how it captures our life together. I am incredibly fortunate for your unwavering love and support, both in life and throughout this process, especially during times of doubt. There's no one I'd rather grow and evolve with, who understands me and cares so deeply for my well-being. I love you so much.

A big thank you to the following ceramists for generously providing the beautiful pieces featured in the book:

- *Wu Ceramics – Mengchao Wu*
- *Haneu Haneu Ceramics*
- *Fingers Crossed Ceramics – Stephanie Alviani*
- *Evything Studio – Eveline Lam*
- *Cathy Terepocki Ceramics*

INDEX